Delights of
Old Montréal

Arts / History / Design / Gastronomy / Discoveries

ULYSSES

Research and Writing
Julie Brodeur, Alexandra Hamel, François Rémillard

Associate Editors
Annie Gilbert, Pierre Ledoux, Nadège Picard

Copy Editing and Translation
Matthew McLauchlin

Graphic Design and Layout
Pascal Biet

Photo Credits
See page 127

This work was produced under the direction of Olivier Gougeon.

Acknowledgements

This book was produced in collaboration with the Société de développement commercial du Vieux-Montréal (SDC). A warm thank you to President Micheal Banks and General Director Daniel Soucy, for their support in this project, and to Krystel Verreault for her valuable help.

We would also like to thank the photographers who took part in the Le Vieux-Montréal en images photo contest. Their beautiful pictures illustrate many of the pages of this book.

We acknowledge the financial support of the Government of Canada through the Book Publishing Industry Development Program (BPIDP) for our publishing activities. We would also like to thank the Government of Québec – Tax credit for book publishing – Administered by SODEC.

Note to Readers

The information contained in this guide was correct at press time. However, mistakes may slip by, omissions are always possible, establishments may move, etc. The authors and publisher hereby disclaim any liability for loss or damage resulting from omissions or errors.

Bibliothèque et Archives nationales du Québec and Library and Archives Canada cataloguing in publication
Main entry under title:
   Delights of Old Montréal : arts, history, design, gastronomy, discoveries
   Translation of: Plaisirs du Vieux-Montréal
   Includes index.
   ISBN 978-2-89464-922-0
   1. Vieux-Montréal (Montréal, Québec) - Guidebooks. 2. Montréal (Québec) - Guidebooks.
FC2947.18.V5313 2009   917.14'28045   C2009-940783-3

Rue Saint-Paul

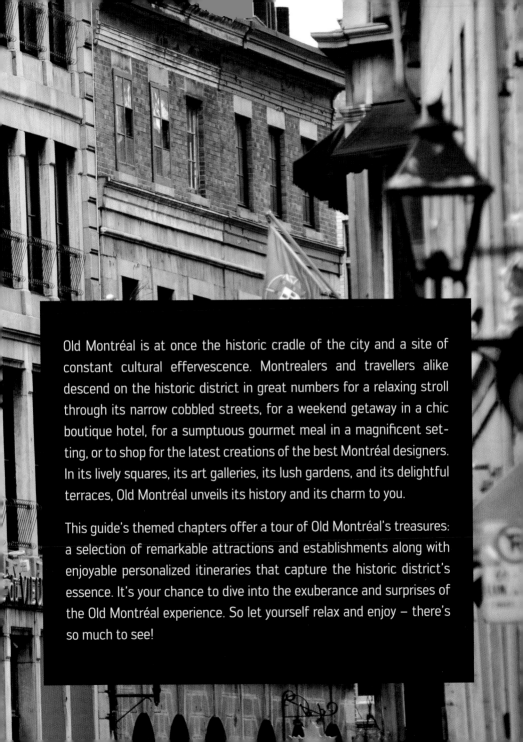

Old Montréal is at once the historic cradle of the city and a site of constant cultural effervescence. Montrealers and travellers alike descend on the historic district in great numbers for a relaxing stroll through its narrow cobbled streets, for a weekend getaway in a chic boutique hotel, for a sumptuous gourmet meal in a magnificent setting, or to shop for the latest creations of the best Montréal designers. In its lively squares, its art galleries, its lush gardens, and its delightful terraces, Old Montréal unveils its history and its charm to you.

This guide's themed chapters offer a tour of Old Montréal's treasures: a selection of remarkable attractions and establishments along with enjoyable personalized itineraries that capture the historic district's essence. It's your chance to dive into the exuberance and surprises of the Old Montréal experience. So let yourself relax and enjoy – there's so much to see!

e Saint-Amable)

Discover

A walking tour winding along the narrow streets of Old Montréal will help you discover this historic and cultural environment, giving you some context for your adventure.

In this chapter, we invite you to soak up the ambiance of this unique neighbourhood and get a glimpse of Old Montréal's spirit and soul by visiting its storied institutions, renowned history museums and architectural landmarks.

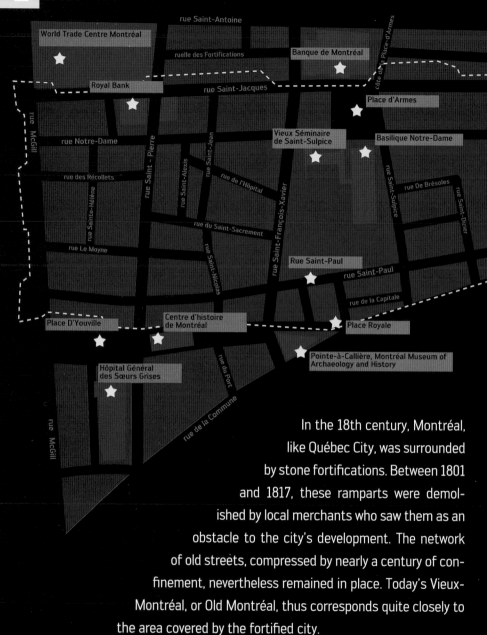

rue Saint-Antoine

World Trade Centre Montréal

ruelle des Fortifications

Banque de Montréal

côte de la Place-d'Armes

boulevard Saint-Laurent

Royal Bank

rue Saint-Jacques

Place d'Armes

rue McGill

rue Notre-Dame

rue Saint-Pierre

Vieux Séminaire de Saint-Sulpice

Basilique Notre-Dame

rue des Récollets

rue Saint-Jean

rue Saint-Alexis

rue de l'Hôpital

rue Saint-Sulpice

rue De Brésoles

rue Saint-Dizier

rue Sainte-Hélène

rue du Saint-Sacrement

rue Saint-François-Xavier

rue Le Moyne

rue Saint-Nicolas

Rue Saint-Paul

rue Saint-Paul

rue de la Capitale

Place D'Youville

Centre d'histoire de Montréal

Place Royale

Hôpital Général des Sœurs Grises

rue du Port

Pointe-à-Callière, Montréal Museum of Archaeology and History

rue de la Commune

rue McGill

In the 18th century, Montréal, like Québec City, was surrounded by stone fortifications. Between 1801 and 1817, these ramparts were demolished by local merchants who saw them as an obstacle to the city's development. The network of old streets, compressed by nearly a century of confinement, nevertheless remained in place. Today's Vieux-Montréal, or Old Montréal, thus corresponds quite closely to the area covered by the fortified city.

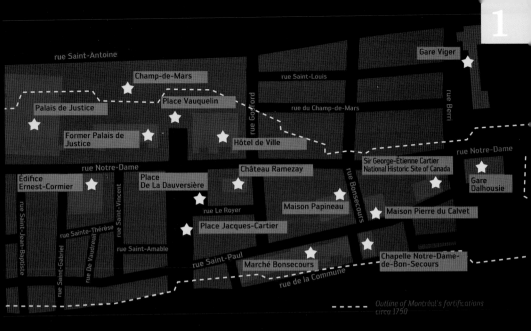

rue Saint-Antoine

Gare Viger

Champ-de-Mars

rue Saint-Louis

Place Vauquelin

rue du Champ-de-Mars

rue Berri

Palais de Justice

rue Gosford

Former Palais de Justice

Hôtel de Ville

rue Notre-Dame

rue Notre-Dame

Sir George-Étienne Cartier National Historic Site of Canada

Édifice Ernest-Cormier

Place De La Dauversière

Château Ramezay

rue Bonsecours

Gare Dalhousie

rue Saint-Jean-Baptiste

rue Saint-Vincent

rue Le Royer

Maison Papineau

Maison Pierre du Calvet

rue Sainte-Thérèse

Place Jacques-Cartier

rue Saint-Gabriel

rue De Vaudreuil

rue Saint-Amable

rue Saint-Paul

Marché Bonsecours

Chapelle Notre-Dame-de-Bon-Secours

rue de la Commune

- - - - - Outline of Montréal's fortifications circa 1750

During the 19th century, this area became the hub of commercial and financial activity in Canada. Banks and insurance companies built sumptuous head offices here, leading to the demolition of almost all the buildings erected under the French Regime.

The area was later largely abandoned for nearly 40 years in favour of today's modern downtown area. Finally, the long process of breathing new life into Old Montréal got underway during the preparations for Expo 67 and continues today with numerous conversion and restoration projects. This revitalization has gotten a second wind since the late 1990s: several high-end hotels have been established in historic buildings, while many Montrealers have rejuvenated the neighbourhood by making it their home.

Now it's your chance to walk the enchanting cobblestone streets and discover Old Montréal's treasures of architecture and history.

The Financial District Tour

This architectural tour of the great head-quarters of Canada's first major financial district begins at the western end of Old Montréal, at the corner of Rue McGill and Rue Saint-Jacques (Square-Victoria metro).

World trade centres are exchange organizations intended to promote international trade. The **World Trade Centre Montréal** *(747 Rue du Square-Victoria; Square-Victoria metro)* lies hidden behind an entire block of old facades. An impressive glassed-in passageway stretches over 180m through the centre of the building, along a portion of **Ruelle des Fortifications**, a lane marking the former location of the northern wall of the fortified city.

Alongside the passageway, visitors will find a fountain and an elegant stone stairway, the setting for a **statue of Amphitirite**, Poseidon's wife, taken from the municipal fountain in Saint-Mihiel-de-la-Meuse, France. This work of art dates back to the mid-18th century; it was created by Barthélémy Guibal, a sculptor from Nîmes, who also designed the fountains gracing Place Stanislas in Nancy. Visitors will also find a portion of the **Berlin Wall**, a gift from the City of Berlin on the occasion of the 350th anniversary of the founding of Montréal.

Rue Saint-Jacques was the main artery of Canadian high finance for over a century.

This role is reflected in its rich and varied architecture, which serves as a veritable encyclopedia of styles from 1830 to 1930. In those years, the country's banks, insurance companies and department stores, as well as its railway and shipping companies, were largely controlled by Montrealers of Scottish extraction who had come to the colonies to make their fortune.

The modern downtown area stands in the background, where glass and steel skyscrapers tower over wide boulevards, marking a sharp contrast with the old part of the city where stone buildings predominate on narrow, compact streets.

Begun in 1928 according to plans by New York skyscraper specialists, the former head office of the **Royal Bank** *(360 Rue St-Jacques; Square-Victoria metro)* was one of the last buildings to be erected during this era of prosperity. The 23-storey tower has a base inspired by Florentine palazzos, which corresponds to the scale of neighbouring buildings. Inside the tower, visitors can admire the high ceilings of this "temple of finance," built at a time when banks needed impressive buildings to win customers' confidence. The walls of the great hall are emblazoned with the heraldic insignia of eight of the 10 Canadian provinces, as well as those of Montréal (St. George's

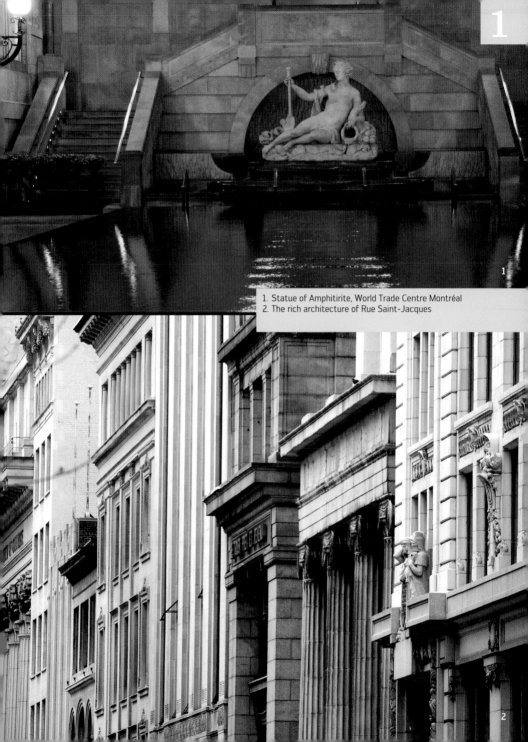

1

1. Statue of Amphitirite, World Trade Centre Montréal
2. The rich architecture of Rue Saint-Jacques

2

1. The former head office of the Royal Bank

COM
U
ASS
CO

Cross) and Halifax (a yellow bird), where the bank was founded in 1861.

The **Molson Bank** *(288 Rue Saint-Jacques; Square-Victoria metro)* was founded in 1854 by the Molson family, famous for the brewery established in 1786 by their ancestor, John Molson (1763-1836). The Molson Bank, like other banks at the time, even printed its own paper money—an indication of the power wielded by its owners, who contributed greatly to the city's development. Completed in 1866, the bank's head office is one of the earliest examples of the Second Empire, or Napoleon III, style to have been erected in Canada. This French style, modelled on the Louvre and the Paris Opera, was extremely popular in North America between 1865 and 1890. Above the entrance, visitors will see the sandstone carvings of the heads of William Molson and two of his children.

Walk along Rue Saint-Jacques; you'll soon reach Place d'Armes.

Under the French Regime, **Place d'Armes** *(Place-d'Armes metro)* was the heart of the city. Used for military manoeuvres and religious processions, the square was also the location of the Gadoys well, the city's main source of potable water. In 1847, the square was transformed into a lovely, fenced-in Victorian garden, which was destroyed at the beginning of the 20th century to make room for a tramway terminal. In the meantime, a **monument to Maisonneuve** was erected

1

1. A Banque de Montréal column
2. Monument to Maisonneuve
3. An Old Montréal horse-drawn carriage's shadow

2

3

in 1895. Executed by sculptor Louis-Philippe Hébert, it shows the founder of Montréal, Paul de Chomedey, Sieur de Maisonneuve, surrounded by prominent figures from the city's early history, namely Jeanne Mance, founder of the Hôtel-Dieu hospital, Lambert Closse and his dog Pilote, and Charles Le Moyne, the head of a family of famous explorers. An Iroquois warrior completes the tableau.

The square, actually a trapezoid, is surrounded by several noteworthy buildings. The **Banque de Montréal** *(119 Rue St-Jacques; Place-d'Armes metro)*, or Bank of Montreal, founded in 1817 by a group of merchants, is the country's oldest banking institution. Its present head office takes up an entire block on the north side of Place d'Armes. A magnificent building created by John Wells in 1847 and modelled after the Roman Pantheon, it has pride of place in the centre of the block. Its Corinthian portico is a monument to the commercial power of the Scottish merchants who founded the institution. The columns' capitals, for their part, were severely damaged by pollution and replaced in 1970 with aluminum replicas. The pediment includes a bas-relief depicting the bank's coat of arms carved out of Binney stone in Scotland by Her Majesty's sculptor, Sir John Steele.

The interior was almost entirely redone in 1904-05. On this occasion, the bank was endowed with a splendid banking hall, designed in the style of a Roman basilica, with green syenite columns, gilded bronze ornamenta-

17

1

tion and beige marble counters. A small **Numismatic Museum** *(free admission; Mon-Fri 10am to 4pm)*, located in the lobby of the more recent building, displays bills from different eras, as well as an amusing collection of mechanical piggy banks. Across from the museum, visitors will find four bas-reliefs carved out of an artificial stone called *coade*, which once graced the facade of the bank's original head office. These were created in 1819, after drawings by English sculptor John Bacon.

The surprising red sandstone **Édifice New York Life** *(511 Place d'Armes)* was erected in 1888 for the insurance company of the same name. Although it only has eight floors, it is regarded as Montréal's first

1. Place d'Armes

skyscraper. The stone used for the facing was imported from Scotland. At the time, this type of stone was transported in the holds of ships, where it served as ballast until it was sold to building contractors at the pier. The neighbouring **Édifice Aldred** *(507 Place-d'Armes)* is adorned with beautiful Art Deco details. It was one of the first buildings over 10 stories to be erected in Montréal after a regulation restricting the height of structures was repealed in 1927.

1. The towers of Basilique Notre-Dame
2. Detail of the square facing the basilica
3. Offering platform and votive candles

Basilique Notre-Dame: An Architectural Masterpiece

2

3

Head for the south side of Place d'Armes to visit the splendid Basilique Notre-Dame and the Vieux Séminaire de Saint-Sulpice.

In 1663, the seigneury of the island of Montréal was acquired by the Sulpicians from Paris, who remained its undisputed masters up until the British conquest of 1759-1760. In addition to distributing land to colonists and laying out the city's first streets, the Sulpicians were responsible for the construction of a large number of buildings, including Montréal's first parish church (1673). Dedicated to *Notre Dame* (Our Lady), this church had a beautiful Baroque facade, which faced straight down the centre of the street of the same name, creating a pleasant perspective characteristic of classical French town planning. At the beginning of the 19th century, however, this rustic little church cut a sorry figure when compared to the Anglican cathedral on Rue Notre-Dame and the new Catholic cathedral on Rue Saint-Denis, neither of which still stands today.

The Sulpicians therefore decided to make a move to surpass their rivals once and for all. In 1823, to the great displeasure of local architects, they commissioned New York architect James O'Donnell, who came from

an Irish Protestant background, to design the largest and most original church north of Mexico.

Basilique Notre-Dame *($5; Mon-Fri 8am to 4:30pm, Sat 8am to 4pm, Sun 12:30pm to 4pm; 110 Rue Notre-Dame Ouest, 514-842-2925 or 866-842-2925, www. basiliquenddm.org; Place-d'Armes metro)*, built between 1824 and 1829, is a true North American masterpiece of Gothic Revival architecture. It should be seen not as a replica of a European cathedral, but rather as a fundamentally neoclassical structure characteristic of the Industrial Revolution, complemented by a medieval-style decor. Note that on Saturdays in summer, visits are limited because of the great number of weddings.

O'Donnell was so pleased with his work that he converted to Catholicism before his death, so that he could be buried under the church. Between 1874 and 1880, the original interior, considered too austere, was replaced by the fabulous polychromatic decorations found today. Executed by Victor Bourgeau, then the leading architect of religious buildings in the Montréal region, along with about 50 artists, it is made entirely of wood, painted and gilded with gold leaf.

Particularly noteworthy features include the baptistery, decorated with frescoes by Ozias Leduc, and the powerful electro-pneumatic Casavant organ with 7,000 pipes, often used during the numerous concerts given at the

1. The polychromatic decor of Basilique Notre-Dame

1. Cours Le Royer
2. Inside Basilique Notre-Dame
3. Vieux Séminaire de Saint-Sulpice

basilica. Lastly, there are the stained-glass windows by Francis Chigot, a master glass artist from France, which depict various episodes in the history of Montréal. They were installed in honour of the church's centennial.

To the right of the chancel, a passage leads to the Chapelle du Sacré-Cœur (Sacred Heart Chapel), added to the back of the church in 1888. Nicknamed *"Chapelle des Mariages"* (Wedding Chapel) because of the countless nuptials held there every year, it was seriously damaged by fire in 1978. The spiral staircases and the side galleries are all that remain of the exuberant, Spanish-style Gothic Revival decor of the original. The architects decided to tie in these vestiges with a modern design, completed in 1981, and included a lovely sectioned vault with skylights, a large bronze reredos by Charles Daudelin and a Guilbault-Thérien mechanical organ.

The **Vieux Séminaire de Saint-Sulpice** *(130 Rue Notre-Dame Ouest; Place-d'Armes metro)*, or old seminary, was built in 1683 in the style of a Parisian *hôtel particulier*, with a courtyard in front and a garden in back. It is the oldest building in the city. For more than three centuries, it has been occupied by Sulpician priests who, under the French Regime, used it as a manor from which they managed their vast seigneury. At the time of the building's construction, Montréal was home to barely 500 inhabitants and was constantly being terrorized by Iroquois attacks. Under those circumstances, the seminary, although

modest in appearance, represented a precious haven of European civilization in the middle of the wilderness. The public clock at the top of the facade was installed in 1701, and may be the oldest one of its kind in the Americas.

The immense warehouses of the **Cours Le Royer** *(corner of Rue St-Sulpice and Rue St-Paul; Place-d'Armes metro)* belonged to the *religieuses hospitalières* (nursing sisters) of Saint-Joseph, who rented them out to importers. Designed between 1860 and 1871 by Michel Laurent and Victor Bourgeau, who seldom worked on commercial structures, they are located on the site of Montréal's first Hôtel-Dieu hospital, founded by Jeanne Mance in 1642. The warehouses, covering a total of 43,000m², were converted into apartments and offices between 1977 and 1986. The small Rue Le Royer was excavated to make room for an underground parking lot, now covered by a lovely pedestrian mall edged with trees and public benches.

Old Montréal features a large number of 19th-century warehouses with stone frames, used to store the goods unloaded from ships at the nearby port. Certain elements of their design—their large glass surfaces, intended to reduce the need for artificial gas lighting and consequently the risk of fire, their wide open interior spaces, the austere style of their Victorian facades—make these buildings the natural precursors of modern architecture. Many of the warehouses have been converted into luxurious hotels.

Experiencing Old Montréal's History Museums

As you visit the major historic sites of Old Montréal, you will come across two of the city's most fascinating museums: Pointe-à-Callière and the Centre d'Histoire de Montréal.

Rue Saint-Paul is Montréal's oldest street. It was drawn by land surveyor Bénigne de Basset in 1672 according to urban planner and historian Dollier de Casson's plans, and was Montréal's main commercial artery for a long time. It is probably Old Montréal's most emblematic street, lined with 19th-century stone buildings that are home to art galleries and arts-and-crafts shops, making it a great place for a stroll. Don't miss Rose-Aimée Bélanger's charming sculpture *Les chuchoteuses* in Placette Saint-Dizier, on Rue Saint-Paul just west of Boulevard Saint-Laurent.

Montréal's oldest public square, **Place Royale** *(Place-d'Armes metro)*, dates back to 1657. Originally a market square, it later became a pretty Victorian garden surrounded by a cast-iron fence. In 1991, it was raised in order to make room for the archaeological crypt of the Pointe-à-Callière museum.

The **Maison de la Douane**, the former customs house, lies on the north side of the Place Royale. It is a lovely example of British neoclassical architecture transplanted into a Canadian setting. The building's austere lines, accentuated by the facing of local grey stone, are offset by the appropriate proportions and simplified references to antiquity. The old customs house was built in 1836 and is now part of the Pointe-à-Callière museum.

The **Pointe-à-Callière, Montréal Museum of Archaeology and History** *($14; Sep to Jun Tue-Fri 10am to 5pm, Sat and Sun 11am to 5pm; Jul and Aug Mon-Fri 10am to 6pm, Sat and Sun 11am to 6pm; 350 Place Royale, 514-872-9150, www.pacmusee.qc.ca; Place-d'Armes metro)* lies on the exact site where Montréal was founded on May 17, 1642: Pointe à Callière. A commemorative obelisk, the *Monument aux pionniers*, was erected in 1893 in the centre of Place D'Youville to commemorate the 250th anniversary of the city's founding the year before. The small Saint-Pierre river used to flow alongside the area now occupied by Place D'Youville, while the muddy banks of the St. Lawrence reached almost as far as the present-day Rue de la Commune where the first colonists built Fort

1

1. Rue Saint-Paul
2. One of the hazards of winter

RUE SAINT-PAUL
EST

2

Ville-Marie. The colony's leaders soon decided to build the city on the opposite bank, where Rue Saint-Paul and Rue Notre-Dame are today; they date back to this period. The site of the fort was then occupied by a cemetery and the château of Governor de Callière, hence the name.

The museum uses the most advanced technologies available to provide visitors with a survey of the city's history. Attractions include a multimedia presentation with conversations with holographic characters, a visit to the vestiges discovered on the site, excellent models illustrating the stages of Place Royale's development, holograms and thematic exhibitions. The museum was established in 1992 to mark the city's 350th anniversary.

Located west of the museum and extending from Place Royale to Rue McGill, **Place D'Youville** owes its elongated shape to its location on top of the bed of the Petite Rivière Saint-Pierre, which was covered in 1832.

1

In the heart of Place D'Youville stands former fire station no. 1, one of Québec's rare examples of Flemish-inspired architecture. The station is now home to the **Centre d'Histoire de Montréal** *($6; Tue-Sun 10am to 5pm; 335 Place D'Youville, 514-872-3207, www.ville.montreal.qc.ca/chm).* A lovely exhibit showcasing various objects relating Montréal's history is presented on the first floor. Thanks to lively presentations, visitors can follow the city's evolution and learn about significant events such as Expo 67, discover daily life in various eras, hear about major strikes in the city and see how several heritage buildings were demolished. Sound recordings in particular play an important role here, with taped interviews with Montrealers of various origins talking about their city. On

1. Pointe-à-Callière, Montréal Museum of Archaeology and History
2. Place D'Youville

1. Centre d'Histoire de Montréal and Place D'Youville
2. Maison de Mère d'Youville

the top floors are temporary exhibits as well as a glass covered overpass from which you can admire Old Montréal.

The Sœurs de la Charité (Sisters of Charity) are better known as the Sœurs Grises (Grey Nuns), a nickname given to these nuns who were falsely accused of selling alcohol to natives and getting them drunk (in French,

gris means both grey and tipsy). In 1747, the founder of the community, Marguerite d'Youville, took charge of the former Hôpital des Frères Charon, established in 1693, and transformed it into the **Hôpital Général des Sœurs Grises** *(138 Rue St-Pierre; Square-Victoria metro)*, a shelter for the city's homeless children. The west wing and the ruins of the chapel are all that remain of this com-

Old Montréal's Cultural and Administrative District

Heading east along Rue de la Commune, you will enjoy a magnificent view of the Old Port and its inviting green spaces.

Originally a strip of land used for animal grazing (1651), **Rue de la Commune** was quickly transformed into an industrial sector. It was only at the start of the 1990s that measures were undertaken to showcase the view of the river and the unique architecture of the neoclassical grey-stone warehouses that stand before the city, one of the few examples of so-called "waterfront planning" in North America.

In 1754, Richard Dulong opened an inn on the narrow Rue Saint-Gabriel. Today, the **Auberge Saint-Gabriel** *(426 Rue St-Gabriel, 514-878-3561; Place-d'Armes metro)*, the

founded about 20 years ago in the former Caserne Saint-Gabriel, the oldest firehouse in Montréal that is still standing. This Victorian-style structure was built in 1871-1872.

No fewer than three courthouses are found along Rue Notre-Dame. Inaugurated in 1971, the massive **Palais de Justice** *(1 Rue Notre-Dame Est; Champ-de-Mars metro)*, or courthouse, dwarfs the surroundings. A sculpture by Charles Daudelin entitled *Allegrocube* stands on its steps. A mechanism makes it possible to open and close this stylized "hand of justice."

From the time it was inaugurated in 1926 until it closed in 1970, the building then known as the "new" courthouse hosted crim-

1. Rue de la Commune
2. Palais de Justice

1

1. Édifice Ernest-Cormier
2. The former Palais de Justice

Édifice Ernest-Cormier is graced with out-standing bronze sconces, cast in Paris at the workshops of Edgar Brandt. Their installation in 1925 ushered in the Art Deco style in Canada. The main hall, faced with travertine and topped by three dome-shaped skylights, is worth a quick visit.

The **former Palais de Justice** *(155 Rue Notre-Dame Est; Champ-de-Mars metro)*, the oldest courthouse in Montréal, was built between 1849 and 1856 on the site of the first courthouse, which was erected in 1800. It is another fine example of Canadian neo-classical architecture. After the courts were divided in 1926, the old Palais was used for civil cases. The building was expanded in 1905 Since the opening of the Palais to its left, the old Palais has been converted into an annex of city hall, located to the right.

As you continue along Rue Notre-Dame, Place Jacques-Cartier will appear on your right.

Place Jacques-Cartier *(Champ-de-Mars metro)* was laid out on the site once occupied by the Château de Vaudreuil, which burned down in 1803. The former Montréal residence of the governor of New France was without question the most elegant private home in the city. Designed by engineer Gaspard Chaussegros de Léry in 1723, it had a horseshoe-shaped staircase leading up to a handsome cut-stone portal, two projecting pavilions (one on each side of the main part of the building), and a formal garden that extended as far as Rue Notre-Dame. The property was purchased by local merchants, who decided to give the government a small strip of land, on the condition that a public market be established there, thus increasing the value of the adjacent property that remained in private hands. This explains Place Jacques-Cartier's oblong shape.

Merchants of British descent sought various means of ensuring their visibility and publicly expressing their patriotism in Montréal. They quickly formed a much larger community in Montréal than in Québec City, where government and military headquarters were located. In 1809, they were the first in the world to erect a monument to Admiral Horatio Nelson, who defeated the combined French and Spanish fleets in the Battle of Trafalgar. Supposedly, they even got French-Canadian merchants drunk in order to extort a financial contribution from them for the project. The base of the **Colonne Nelson**, or Nelson Column, was designed and executed in London. It is decorated with bas-relief depicting the exploits of the famous admiral at Abukir, Copenhagen and, of course, Trafalgar. The statue of Nelson at the top was originally made of an artificial type of stone, but after being damaged time and time again by protestors, it was finally replaced by a fibreglass replica in 1981. The column is the oldest extant monument in Montréal.

At the other end of Place Jacques-Cartier, visitors will see the Quai Jacques-Cartier

1

and the river, while **Rue Saint-Amable** lies tucked away on the right, at the halfway mark. In summer, artists and artisans gather on this little street, selling jewellery, drawings, etchings and caricatures.

Under the French Regime, Montréal, following the example of Québec City and Trois-Rivières, had its own governor, not to be

1. A shop on Place Jacques-Cartier
2. Screen prints for sale

confused with the governor of New France. The situation was the same under the English Regime. It wasn't until 1833 that the first elected mayor, Jacques Viger (1787-1858), took control of the city. This man, who was passionate about history, gave Montréal its motto (*Concordia Salus*, meaning "salvation through harmony") and coat of arms, composed of the four symbols of the "founding" peoples, namely the French-Canadian beaver (since replaced by the fleur-de-lys), the Irish clover, the Scottish thistle and the English rose.

After occupying a number of inadequate buildings for decades (a notable example was the Hayes aqueduct, an edifice containing an immense reservoir of water, which one day cracked while a meeting was being held in the council chamber just below), the municipal administration finally moved into its present home in 1878. The **Hôtel de Ville** *(275 Rue Notre-Dame Est; Champ-de-Mars metro)*, or city hall, a fine example of the Second Empire, or Napoleon III, style, is the work of Henri-Maurice Perrault, who also designed the neighbouring courthouse. In 1922, a fire destroyed the interior and roof of the building, which was later restored in 1926 on the model of the city hall in Tours, France. Exhibitions are occasionally presented in the main hall, which is accessible via the main entrance. It was from the balcony of this building that France's General de Gaulle

cried out his famous "*Vive le Québec libre!*" ("Long live a free Québec!") in 1967, to the great delight of the crowd gathered in front of the building.

Head to the rear of the Hôtel de Ville by way of the lovely **Place Vauquelin**, the continuation of Place Jacques-Cartier. Created in 1930 by French sculptor Paul-Eugène Bénet, a native of Dieppe, the statue of Admiral Jean Vauquelin (1728-1772), defender of Louisbourg at the end of the French Regime, was probably put here to counterbalance the monument to Nelson, a symbol of British control over Canada.

Go down the staircase leading to the **Champ-de-Mars**, modified in 1991 in order to reveal some vestiges of the fortifications that once surrounded Montréal. Gaspard Chaussegros de Léry designed Montréal's ramparts, erected between 1717 and 1745, as well as those of Québec City. The walls of Montréal, however, never saw conflict, as the city's commercial calling and location discouraged assault. The large, tree-lined lawns are reminders of the Champ-de-Mars' former vocation as a parade ground for military manoeuvres until 1924. A view of the downtown area's skyscrapers opens up through the clearing.

Facing City Hall, back on the south side of Rue Notre-Dame, is the beautiful **Place De La Dauversière**. It bears the name of

1. Hôtel de Ville and Place Jacques-Cartier

Jérôme Le Royer de La Dauvèrsière (1597-1659), founder of the Société de Notre-Dame, which sponsored the founding of Montréal. The small park is home to several works of public art, notably the statue of one of Montréal's former mayors, Jean Drapeau. The popular Mayor Drapeau reigned over "his" city for nearly 30 years.

The **Château Ramezay Museum** *($9; Tue-Sun 10am to 4:30pm, summer every day 10am to 6pm; 280 Rue Notre-Dame Est, 514-861-3708, www.chateauramezay.qc.ca; Champ-de-Mars metro)* is located in the humblest of all the "châteaux" built in Montréal, and the only one still standing. Château Ramezay was built in 1705 for the governor of Montréal, Claude de Ramezay, and his family. In 1745, it fell into the hands of the Compagnie des Indes Occidentales (The French West Indies Company), which rebuilt it in 1756. Valuable Canadian furs were stored in its vaults awaiting shipment to France. After the conquest, British merchants occupied the house, before being temporarily supplanted by American insurgents who wanted the province of Québec to join the nascent United States. Benjamin Franklin even stayed at the château for a few months in 1775, in an attempt to convince Montrealers to become American citizens.

In 1895, after serving as the first building of the Montréal branch of the Université Laval in Québec City, the château was converted into a museum, under the patronage of the Société d'Archéologie et de Numismatique de Montréal, founded by Jacques Viger. Visitors can admire a rich collection of paintings and European, Canadian and Aboriginal artifacts dating from the pre-Columbian era to the early 20th century. The Salle de Nantes is decorated with beautiful Louis XV-style mahogany panelling, designed around 1725 by Germain Boffrand and imported from the Nantes office of the Compagnie des Indes Occidentales.

In addition to its permanent and temporary exhibits, the museum organizes outside workshops and a variety of cultural activities. The Château Ramezay itself is adorned by the beautiful **Jardin du Gouverneur**, a French-style garden similar to typical Montréal gardens of the 18th century. It contains the Café du Château and the Marie-Charlotte boutique.

1. Rue Le Royer, behind the Château Ramezay
2. The silhouette of the Hôtel de Ville
3. Statue of Jean Drapeau on Place De La Dauversière

The East End of Old Montréal: Off the Beaten Path

A bit off of the tourist track and away from the pedestrian crowds, this part of the district contains a number of intriguing historic attractions.

At the corner of Rue Berri and Rue Notre-Dame stands the **Sir George-Étienne Cartier National Historic Site of Canada** *($3.90; early Sep to late Dec and early Apr to late May Wed-Sun 10am to noon and 1pm to 5pm; late May to early Sep every day 10am to 6pm; closed Jan to Mar; 458 Rue Notre-Dame Est, 514-283-2282 or 888-773-8888, www.pc.gc.ca/cartier; Champ-de-Mars metro)*, consisting of two adjoining houses inhabited successively by George-Étienne Cartier, one of the Fathers of Canadian Confederation. Inside, visitors will find a reconstructed mid-19th-century French-Canadian bourgeois home. Interesting educational soundtracks accompany the tour and add a touch of authenticity to the site.

The neighbouring building, at number 452, is the former **Cathédrale Schismatique Grecque Saint-Nicolas**, built around 1910 in the Romanesque-Byzantine Revival style.

Rue Berri marks the eastern border of Old Montréal, and thus the fortified city of the French Regime, beyond which extended the Faubourg Québec, excavated in the 19th century to make way for railroad lines. This explains the sharp difference in height between the hill known as Côteau Saint-Louis and the Viger and Dalhousie stations.

Gare Viger, visible on the left, was inaugurated by Canadian Pacific in 1897 in order to serve the eastern part of the country. Its resemblance to the Château Frontenac in Québec City is not a coincidence; both buildings were designed for the same railroad company and by the same architect, an American named Bruce Price. The Château-style station, which closed in 1935, also included a prestigious hotel and large stained-glass train shed that has since been demolished.

The smaller **Gare Dalhousie** *(514 Rue Notre-Dame Est; Champ-de-Mars metro)*, located near the Maison Cartier, was the first railway station built by Canadian Pacific, a company established for the purpose of building a Canadian transcontinental railroad. The station was the starting point of the first transcontinental train headed for Port Moody (20km from Vancouver) on June 28, 1886.

For a long time, Gare Dalhousie was home to the École Nationale de Cirque de Montréal, which recently moved to a building located in what is now known as TOHU, la Cité des Arts du Cirque, in the northern part of the Island of Montréal. The Éloize circus company has since taken its place.

From Rue Notre-Dame, the port's former refrigerated warehouse, made of brown brick, is visible, as well as Île Sainte-Hélène, in the middle of the river. This island, along with Île Notre-Dame, was the site of Expo 67.

1. Rue Saint-Louis
2. Gare Viger
3. Square Dalhousie

1. Rue Saint-Paul
2. A votive offering in the shape of a ship inside Chapelle Notre-Dame-de-Bon-Secours

The Architectural Heritage Around Marché Bonsecours

From Rue Berri, turn right on Rue Saint-Paul which offers a lovely view of the Marché Bonsecours dome. Continue straight ahead to Chapelle Notre-Dame-de-Bon-Secours.

This site was originally occupied by another chapel, built in 1658 upon the recommendation of Saint Marguerite Bourgeoys, founder of the congregation of Notre-Dame. The present **Chapelle Notre-Dame-de-Bon-Secours** *(400 Rue St-Paul Est; Champ-de-Mars metro)* dates back to 1771, when the Sulpicians wanted to establish a branch of the main parish in the eastern part of the fortified city. In 1890, the chapel was modified to suit contemporary tastes, and the present stone facade was added, along with the "aerial" chapel (1893-1894) looking out on the port. Parishioners asked for God's blessing on ships and crews bound for Europe from this chapel. The interior, redone at the same time, contains a large number of votive offerings from sailors saved from shipwrecks. Some are in the form of model ships, hung from the ceiling of the nave. The chapel now hosts a variety of concerts and other activities in partnership with the Musée Marguerite-Bourgeoys.

Between 1996 and 1998, excavations below the chapel's nave uncovered several pre-

Discover

historic Aboriginal artifacts. Today, the **Musée Marguerite-Bourgeoys** *($8; May to Oct Tue-Sun 10am to 5:30pm, Nov to mid-Jan and Mar-Apr Tue-Sun 11am to 3:30pm, closed mid-Jan to Feb; 400 Rue St-Paul Est, 514-282-8670, www.marguerite-bourgeoys. com; Champ-de-Mars metro)* displays these interesting archaeological finds. But there is even more to explore: adjoining the Notre-Dame-de-Bon-Secours chapel, it leads from the top of the tower, where the view is breath-taking, to the depths of the crypt, where the old stones tell their own story. Learn about the life of Marguerite Bourgeoys, a pioneer of education in Québec, admire her portrait and discover the mystery surrounding her. Guided tours of the archaeological site surrounding the foundations of the stone chapel, the oldest in Montréal, are offered.

The **Maison Pierre du Calvet**, at the corner of Rue Bonsecours (no. 401), was built in 1725 and is representative of 18th-century French urban architecture adapted to the local setting, with thick walls made of fieldstone embedded in mortar, storm windows doubling the casement windows with their little squares of glass imported from France, and high fire-break walls, then required by local regulations as a means of limiting the spread of fire from one building to the next. One of Montréal's best hostelries, Hostellerie Pierre du Calvet, has occupied the house for many years.

A little higher on Rue Bonsecours, visitors will find the **Maison Papineau** *(440 Rue*

1

3

1. Musée Marguerite-Bourgeoys
2. An Old Montréal cobblestone street
3. Maison Pierre du Calvet

1. Marché Bonsecours

Bonsecours; Champ-de-Mars metro), long ago home to Louis-Joseph Papineau (1786-1871), lawyer, politician and head of the French-Canadian nationalist movement until the insurrection of 1837. Built in 1785 and covered with a wooden facing made to look like cut stone, it was one of the first buildings in Old Montréal to be restored (1962).

The **Marché Bonsecours** *(300 Rue St-Paul Est, www.marchebonsecours.qc.ca; Champ-de-Mars metro)* was erected between 1845 and 1850. The lovely grey-stone neoclassical edifice with sash windows is located between Rue Saint-Paul and Rue de la Commune. The building is adorned with a portico supported by cast-iron columns moulded in England, and topped by a silvery dome, which for many years served as the symbol of the city at the entrance to the port. The public market, closed in the early 1960s following the advent of the supermarket, was transformed into municipal offices, then an exhibition hall, before finally partially reopening in 1996. The market now presents an exhibition and features arts-and-crafts shops. The building originally housed both the city hall and a concert hall upstairs. The market's old storehouses, recently renovated, can be seen on Rue Saint-Paul. From the large balcony on Rue de la Commune, you can see the partially reconstructed Bonsecours dock, where paddle-wheelers, full of farmers who came to the city to sell their produce, used to moor.

1. Chapelle Notre-Dame-de-Bon-Secours

2

3

1. Rue Saint-François-Xavier
2. Detail, Édifice Ernest-Cormier
3. Rue Saint-Paul
4. The glass passageway of the World Trade Centre Montréal

4

1. Canadian Bank of Commerce, Rue Saint-Jacques
2. Édifice Exchange Bank, Rue Notre-Dame
3. National Bank tower, Place d'Armes

1. Édifice Aldred
2. A residential loft
3. Édifice Grand Tronc on Rue McGill

(St Paul Hôtel)

Sleep

A haven for lovers' getaways and serious travellers who appreciate comfort and aesthetics, Old Montréal's inns and boutique
hotels compete with each other in beauty and originality. Numerous historic buildings, creatively and daringly restored, have
been converted into high-end hotels that will satisfy the most
exacting guest. Our listings describe the colour and personal-
ity of each of these establishments, so you can experience the
magic of a night in the heart of Old Montréal.

Prices start at $200 (before taxes) for a standard room for two people during peak season.

1

Boutique Hotels

Hôtel Gault

Hôtel Gault is a small, 30-room hotel reminiscent of a private mansion. One could get used to living here! It features designer furnishings and accessories custom-made for its innovative decor. The lobby features large windows that give a feeling of space, and there is a cozy reading nook at the rear. A communal breakfast is served at a large table. All the rooms, occupying four floors, share a similar contemporary style. With the exception of the lofts, the rooms are not very big, but the space is well designed and very comfortable. The lovely, modern bathrooms are equipped with tubs, a heated floor and all the amenities you need to pamper yourself. Some rooms have a patio, and all windows open onto the street and the pretty flower boxes that enhance the facade.

449 Rue Ste-Hélène, 514-904-1616 or
866-904-1616, www.hotelgault.com

Le Saint-Sulpice

Enter the huge lobby of the Saint-Sulpice hotel and discover a world of luxury and comfort with a touch of Old Montréal. Throughout the establishment, decorative elements remind guests that the site is steeped in history: amber-coloured mahogany woodwork, stone walls, rugs with fleur-de-lys

1. Le Saint-Sulpice
2. Hôtel Gault
3. Hôtel Gault

motifs, a fireplace, etc. After all, the Sulpicians played a major role in the city's history; in fact, their basilica and seminary are located next door to the hotel, whose courtyard features a fountain and offers direct access to the beautiful Jardin des Sulpiciens. Because it is an all-suite hotel (there are 108), you will have enough room to move around and a kitchenette to boot. Best of all, some of the suites have a balcony or a roof patio.

414 Rue St-Sulpice, 514-288-1000 or 877-785-7423, www.lesaintsulpice.com

Hôtel Nelligan

It's anyone's guess what the famous poet would have thought of the luxury hotel bearing his name, but one thing's for sure: this place is something else. This boutique hotel boasts 60 well-equipped, very comfortable rooms and suites. The establishment belongs to a family that owns many others in the neighbourhood and, as such, has the know-how to make a place special. Between the lobby and the restaurant is a lovely inner courtyard where breakfast is served. Some of the rooms overlook the courtyard, which, although it lacks a view, makes for a quieter environment. The rooms are attractive, with stone and/or brick walls, wood blinds, modern bathrooms (some of which feature a double whirlpool) and down-filled duvets. Fittingly, a poetry theme can be found throughout the hotel; for instance, the rooms are decorated

1. Hôtel Nelligan
2. Hôtel XIXᵉ Siècle
3. St Paul Hôtel

with canvases on which Nelligan's poems have been handwritten. A complimentary continental breakfast is served in the morning. Note that Hôtel Nelligan's guests have access to the spa in the nearby Place d'Armes hotel.

106 Rue St-Paul Ouest, 514-788-2040 or 877-788-2040, www.hotelnelligan.com

Le Place d'Armes Hôtel & Suites

Among the new boutique hotels that have taken over Old Montréal, one of the first to open was the Place d'Armes, standing at the corner of the square of the same name and facing the magnificent Notre-Dame basilica. The establishment's

136 rooms are spread out over three sections where the decor varies from elegant dark woodwork to rich cream tones and brick walls. Equipped with CD and DVD players, home-movie theatres and modern bathrooms, all rooms are comfortable and practical.

55 Rue St-Jacques, 514-842-1887 or 888-450-1887, www.hotelplacedarmes.com

St Paul Hôtel

The St Paul Hôtel's 96 rooms and 24 suites are housed in a superb historic building that has been entirely renovated. Consequently, the interior decor is very modern, and various materials blend

harmoniously to create a stunning effect. With alabaster and fire, fur and vinyl, black tiling and cream-coloured fabrics, each room has been created with utmost care. The result is an audacious, avant-garde design, a unique place for wealthy, fashionable guests. Despite the bold decor, some of the spaces are quite warm and inviting. For example, in some rooms, the bed area is delimited by a curtain that lends a cozy effect. And if the mood strikes, unwind with a massage in your room.

355 Rue McGill, 514-380-2222 or 866-380-2202, www.hotelstpaul.com

Hôtel XIXe Siècle

Housed in a former bank of Second Empire architecture, the Hôtel XIXe Siècle has both old-fashioned charm and modern attributes. Its 59 rooms are spacious, and high ceilings and large windows add to this feeling of grandeur. Warm hues, stylish furnishings, lovely fabrics and gorgeous bathrooms provide each room with a cozy, comfortable decor. There is also Internet access. The breakfast room dazzles in black and white, while the lobby features armchairs and books to welcome visitors.

262 Rue St-Jacques, 514-985-0019 or 877-553-0019, www.hotelxixsiecle.com

Charming Inns

Les Passants du Sans Soucy

Les Passants du Sans-Soucy is a lovely inn, set in the heart of the old city, whose nine charming rooms are furnished with antiques. Built in 1723, the building was renovated during the 1990s. It offers nine charming rooms with stone walls, exposed beams, and fireplaces. Excellent breakfasts.

171 Rue St-Paul Ouest, 514-842-2634,
www.lesanssoucy.com

Auberge Bonaparte

Well known for its delicious French cuisine, the Bonaparte restaurant features a 30-room inn on its upper floors. All the rooms are quite comfortable and feature a lovely decor as well as Internet access. The rooms at the rear of the build-ing, which dates from 1886, overlook the Jardin des Sulpiciens, behind the Basilique Notre-Dame. Breakfast is served in the restaurant.

447 Rue St-François-Xavier, 514-844-1448,
www.bonaparte.ca

Hostellerie Pierre du Calvet

This establishment is set in one of Montréal's oldest homes (1725), discreetly tucked away at the intersection of Bonsecours and Saint-Paul streets. It has been entirely renovated, as have many other older houses in the neighbourhood. The ten rooms, each with a fireplace, are decorated with lovely antique wood panelling accentuated by stained glass and beautiful antiques. Furnishings include canopy beds and mahogany armoires

1. Hostellerie
   Pierre du Calvet

2. Auberge
   du Vieux-Port

with gold leaf; the bathrooms are tiled in Italian marble. A pretty indoor courtyard and day room allow guests to escape from the crowds. Breakfast is served in a lovely Victorian greenhouse, and service is attentive and meticulous. This inn, located in the heart of the city's historic district, is a real gem that will make your stay absolutely unforgettable. The hotel also hosts the excellent Les Filles du Roy restaurant.

405 Rue Bonsecours, 514-282-1725 or
866-544-1725, www.pierreducalvet.ca

Auberge du Vieux-Port

The Auberge du Vieux-Port is a real gem. It occupies a historic building dating from 1882 whose stone walls have been left exposed in the chic, attractively decorated lobby. The building's construction and the way the rooms are divided highlight its many wood beams and stone walls. The 27 rooms and lofts have been decorated to pay tribute to the past, with outstanding results. There is also a French restaurant in the basement, Narcisse Bistro + Bar à vin, where you can see a segment of the fortifications of the old city. The inn hides another surprise: two romantic terraces connected with Narcisse, including one on the roof, offer guests a splendid view of the river and Rue de la Commune

97 Rue de la Commune Est, 514-876-0081 or
888-660-7678, www.aubergeduvieuxport.com

1. InterContinental Montréal
2. Hôtel Le St-James
3. Hôtel Le St-James

Luxury Hotels

InterContinental Montréal

This hotel, located on the edge of Old Montréal, is linked to the World Trade Centre Montréal and several shops. The Palais des Congrès (convention centre) is right nearby. The hotel has an original look thanks to its turret with multiple windows, where the suites' living rooms are located. The 357 rooms are tastefully decorated with simple furniture. Each one is equipped with a spacious bathroom, among other nice touches. Business people will enjoy all the necessary services, such as computer hook-ups, fax machines and photocopiers. Service is attentive and professional.

360 Rue St-Antoine Ouest, 514-987-9900 or 800-361-3600, www.montreal.intercontinental.com

Hôtel Le St-James

Canada's most chic hotel, Le Saint-James caters to a well-off clientele who wish to explore Montréal while enjoying a comfortable stay in a sumptuous, refined environment. Alongside all the modern conveniences and business technologies, its lobby, halls, rooms, and suites are furnished with hand-picked furnishings, antiques, paintings, and sculptures. The building's architecture, with its friezes and mouldings, is accentuated by the warmth and richness of the decor.

355 Rue St-Jacques, 514-841-3111 or 866-841-3111, www.hotellestjames.com

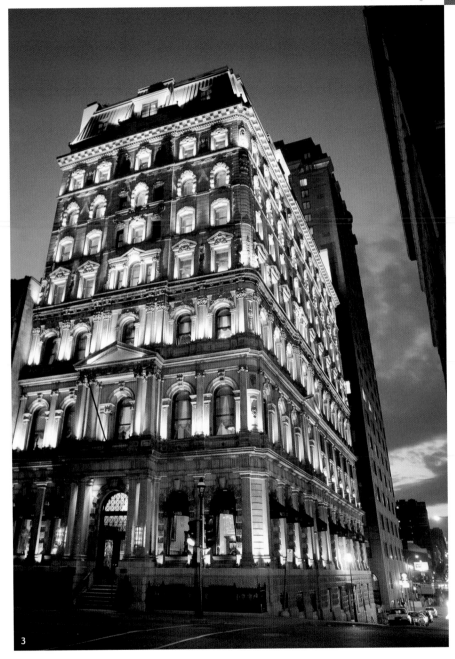

3

(Le Club Chasse et Pêche)

Eat

Treating yourself to a sumptuous dinner is definitely one of the main pleasures of Old Montréal, home to hundreds of the city's best restaurants. We've chosen some of the most exceptional, refined establishments with a range of ambiances and delicious cuisines. Whether by the finesse and savoir-faire of their menus, their audacious decor, or their luxurious terraces, each of these restaurants stands out from the pack. To help you choose, we've divided the offerings between charming and unique places for a quick lunch, chic new bistros, and sumptuous local institutions.

Prices in this guide are for a meal for one person, excluding drinks, taxes and tip.
**$** *less than 15$*   **$$** *15$ to 25$*   **$$$** *26$ to 50$*   **$$$$** *more than 50$*

On The Go

Crémerie Saint-Vincent

Only open in the summertime, the Crémerie Saint-Vincent is one of the few spots in Montréal where you can enjoy delicious maple sugar soft ice cream. The menu features a wide variety of flavours.

153 Rue St-Paul Est, 514-392-2540 **$**

Les Glaceurs

This colourful little ice cream parlour, little more than a few tables and a counter, offers a marvellous array of homemade cupcakes, as well as sorbets and ice creams from Montréal's beloved Glacier Bilboquet, coffee, and sandwiches.

453 Rue St-Sulpice, 514-504-1469, www.lesglaceurs.ca **$**

Ming Tao Xuan

A delightful vacation in a vacation, this authentic tea house and tea ware boutique, run by a couple from Hong Kong, is decorated with Asian treasures presided over by a splendid statue of the Buddha. Hand-carved wood shelves display a collection of fine teapots, teacups and traditional Chinese figurines. Three intimate spaces welcome customers for tea. The proprietors will perform a tea ceremony on request for no extra charge.

451 Rue St-Sulpice, 514-845-9448 **$**

Olive + Gourmando

This Rue Saint-Paul bistro's two owners used to ply their trade at Toqué, one of the city's most

1. Ming Tao Xuan
2. Nomad Station
3. Marché Serafim

famous restaurants. Start your meal off with the exquisite soup of the day, then move on to a delicious salad served with a smoked-trout sandwich, and top it all off with their famous brownies flavoured with Illy coffee. You won't be disappointed! This charming bistro is a good choice for an unpretentious gourmet meal.
351 Rue St-Paul Ouest, 514-350-1083, www.oliveetgourmando.com **$$**

Beniamino

A Rue McGill institution, Benianimo is both a market selling basic groceries and fine foods and a counter selling delicious prepared meals both to eat in and take out. Each day brings new Italian dishes and the best paninis in town.
32 Rue McGill, 514-284-1711 **$**

Titanic

Titanic is a very busy lunch spot located in a semi-basement. During the week days, it offers a multitude of baguette sandwiches and Mediterranean-style salads, feta and other cheeses, smoked fish, pâtés, and marinated vegetables, all delicious.
445 Rue St-Pierre, 514-849-0894 **$**

Nomad Station

Dominated by an amazing mural combining fantastic characters from comic books, Nomad Station café is part of an ongoing media arts project. In this luminous restaurant, clients can snack from 8am to 4pm (sandwiches, pizzas, calzones, gelato, and a selection of candy), enjoy fair-trade coffee, and cast their eyes over a panoply

1 2

of postcard-like small screens on the wall that play looped short films by artists from all over the world. Touch screens give access to all the films.
407 Rue McGill, Suite 105, 514-844-7979, www.nomadmoments.tv **$**

Marché Serafim

It's a treat to sit down at the counter in the delightful chaos of Marché Sérafim. This organic food store also sells organic breakfasts and snacks.
393 Rue St-Paul Est, 514-861-8181 **$**

Stew Stop

Stew Stop's original concept made it Canada's first completely organic boutique restaurant, offering a galaxy of gourmet products and delicious hot dishes. You can enjoy its daily selection of comfort food, both vegan (chili, tofu Marengo) and with meat (lemon turmeric pork, Cuban *picadillo*), in a relaxing environment, along with wine by the glass or the bottle.
372 Rue St-Paul Ouest, 514-303-0370, www.stewstop.ca **$$**

1. Stew Stop
2. Olive + Gourmando
3. Marché de la Villette

Friendly Bistros

Marché de la Villette
A stop at Marché de la Villette for a snack or to buy some of its divine cheeses and deli meats is an experience in itself. The surprising but cozy decor and the loud French music create a delightfully kitschy atmosphere. For a casual lunch, enjoy one of their great sandwiches or cheap, delicious comfort food.
324 Rue St-Paul Ouest, 514-807-8084 **$**

L'Arrivage
L'Arrivage restaurant in the Pointe-à-Callière museum offers a delectable and surprisingly affordable table d'hôte. The second-floor restaurant's large windows offer a magnificent view of the Old Port.
350 Place Royale, 514-872-9128,
www.pacmusee.qc.ca **$-$$**

Gandhi
The sober, well-lit decor and the dishes from the purest traditions of Indian cuisine make this a jewel in Old Montréal's gastronomic crown. The tandooris are especially recommended.
230 Rue St-Paul Ouest, 514-845-5866,
www.restaurantgandhi.com **$$**

Casa de Matéo
Decorated with hammocks, cacti and Latin-American knick-knacks, Casa de Matéo is a delightful Mexican restaurant. The restaurant's staff will be glad to help you bone up on your rusty Spanish, while the food is authentic and delicious.
440 Rue St-François-Xavier, 514-844-7448,
www.casademateo.com **$$**

Jardin Nelson

All summer long, diners flock to the magnificent terrace of the Jardin Nelson for unpretentious treats from a simple menu of crepes and pizzas or for a refreshing sangria. The lush environment of flowers and greenery is a perfect setting for the daily jazz concerts.

407 Place Jacques-Cartier, 514-861-5731, www.jardinnelson.com **$$**

Stash Café

This charming little Polish restaurant with a simple, cozy decor is the ideal choice for delicious cheese-stuffed pierogies, sausage and sauerkraut. The vodka is also excellent.

200 Rue St-Paul Ouest, 514-845-6611, www.stashcafe.com **$$**

Boris Bistro

Boris Bistro regulars will probably tell you that they come to this restaurant for the setting: the two-storey terrace provides this eatery with lots of charm. Simple, unassuming bistro-style fare and a laid-back atmosphere are the other reasons why they flock here for lunch.

465 Rue McGill, 514-848-9575, www.borisbistro.com **$$$**

La Gargote

La Gargote is not what you would expect from its name, which means "a cheap place to eat" in French. Rather, it is a small French restaurant that attracts a regular clientele and curious newcomers. The decor is inviting, the cuisine tasty and the prices affordable.

351 Place D'Youville, 514-844-1428, www.bar-resto.com/gargote **$$$**

1. Casa de Matéo
2. Jardin Nelson
3. Boris Bistro

Le Petit Moulinsart

An Old Montréal institution for more than 20 years, Le Petit Moulinsart is a Belgian bistro that could easily pass for a small museum devoted to the characters of the *Tintin* comic books. The menu includes a number of Walloon and Flemish specialties and, of course, good Belgian beers. *139 Rue St-Paul Ouest, 514-843-7432, www.lepetitmoulinsart.com* **$$$**

Modavie

You will recognize Modavie by the awning above its windows. Its beautiful decor, both modern and antique, creates a soothing atmosphere. Mediterranean-style dishes are served here, as delicious as the nightly jazz concerts. *1 Rue St-Paul Ouest, 514-287-9582, www.modavie.com* **$$$**

Restaurant Le Fripon

One of the rare restaurants on Place Jacques-Cartier to open in winter, Le Fripon offers varied French cuisine heavy on game and seafood. Its two terraces (interior and exterior) and the distinct atmospheres of its two dining rooms (the main dining room and the bistro) please both gourmets and visitors who want a bite to eat while watching the comings and goings on Place Jacques-Cartier. *436 Place Jacques-Cartier, 514-861-1386, www.lefripon.com* **$$$$**

Holder

Both chic and friendly, this European-style *brasserie* has become a mainstay of Rue McGill. The warm colours and leather benches offer a warm, casual environment for the lively crowd

1. Holder
2. Stuzzichi
3. Le Bourlingueur

that descends on the bar for *cinq à sept* (cocktail hour), sitting down to delicious bistro-style cooking. A sumptuous brunch is also available. *407 Rue McGill, 514-849-0333, www.restaurantholder.com* **$$$**

Tatami Sushi Bar & Grill

Sushi lovers should not miss the chance to treat themselves to the delicious rolls and sets prepared with finesse and creativity. The menu isn't all that's innovative in this tranquil restaurant – the furniture will surprise and delight young and old with the tanks of brilliant tropical fish serving as tables. Good value.

140 Rue Notre-Dame Ouest, 514-845-5864 **$$$**

Le Bourlingueur

If you've had enough of trendy restaurants with ultramodern décor, Le Bourlingueur is the antidote. A convivial spot to enjoy with the family, it offers French cuisine punctuated by Alsatian specialties. Its fans appreciate its unpretentious menu and its warm welcome.

363 Rue St-François-Xavier, 514-845-3646, www.lebourlingueur.ca **$$$**

Le Cabaret du Roy

If you plan on dining at this restaurant, don't expect an ordinary night out. After all, you're at Cabaret du Roy, and you're not alone. A crowd of characters right out of Montréal's golden age awaits diners in an old-fashioned decor and involves them in an entertaining historical re-enactment. Rest assured, you don't have to participate if you don't feel like it. You might not learn the city's entire history in one night, but the entertainment is worthwhile—not to mention the food. Traditional dishes with a twist make up a fantastic menu. Storytelling evenings on Sunday.

Bonsecours Market, 363 Rue de la Commune Est, 514-907-9000, www.oyez.ca **$$$**

Stuzzichi

Stuzzichi (from *stuzzicare* 'to whet the appetite') offers friendly service in an ingeniously decorated setting. Its specialty is tapas, best shared between friends.

358 Rue Notre-Dame Est, 514-759-0505 **$$$$**

1. Chez l'Épicier
2. Barroco

Chic and Trendy

Le Cartet

Warm and sunny Le Cartet starts with a display of prepared dishes and sandwiches, as well as fine groceries including a vast selection of chocolates. In the restaurant section, customers share two large wooden tables (smaller tables are also available) for lively weekend brunches, a delicious coffee, or affordable and savoury bistro-type meals.

106 Rue McGill, 514-871-8887 **$$**

Chez l'Épicier

This is a wonderful spot to savour fresh products and market-inspired cuisine. L'Épicier ("the grocer"), which doubles as a gourmet store, is first and foremost a restaurant that serves good, creative food in spectacular style. Stone walls, large windows overlooking the magnificent architecture of the Bonsecours Market and a bistro-style decor give the place an atmosphere that is both lively and intimate. L'Épicier's wine bar also features some interesting selections.

311 Rue St-Paul Est, 514-878-2232,
www.chezlepicier.com **$$$**

Restaurant Vallier

This classy cantina serves favourites of Québec cuisine in an impressive decor made from reclaimed materials, such as vintage furniture and lamps from the 1950s and 1960s. Along with comfort food such as shepherd's pie made from duck confit and cheese and bacon macaroni, the

2

menu features bistro-style dishes and excellent hamburgers.
425 Rue McGill, 514-842-2905, www.restaurantvallier.com **$$$**

Méchant Bœuf Bar et Brasserie

A perfect spot for a late-night snack, Le Méchant Bœuf draws its inspiration from British gastropubs and French bistros. Touches of brilliant red and the rustling of a mural waterfall enhance the carefully designed decor. The menu features large, delicious hamburgers and a panoply of mouthwatering tartares, beer chicken, and perfectly prepared fish, served with microbrewery beers in a relaxed, lively ambiance.
124 Rue St-Paul Ouest, 514-788-4020, www.mechantboeuf.com **$$$**

Aziatik

In a modern decor with imitation crocodile-skin benches and huge cross-shaped lamps made of wood and mirrors, Aziatik offers fine Asian cuisine (teriyaki, curry, sushi, etc.) in a trendy atmosphere.
626 Rue Marguerite-D'Youville, 514-843-8388, www.aziatik.ca **$$$**

Barroco

Barroco's clientele enjoy copious dishes of rustic French and Spanish comfort food, simmered or braised. As the name suggests, the decor is both chic and welcoming, with elegant tables set with mismatched dishes. The bar serves excellent cocktails. Very lively on weekends, when a DJ starts pumping out the decibels.
312 Rue St-Paul Ouest, 514-544-5800 **$$$**

1. S Le Restaurant
2. Aszú
3. Vauvert

Õra Resto-bar

With its white leather armchairs and its candy-coloured neon lights, Õra's decor, like its cuisine, is inspired by the sea. The menu is a creative selection of the best Mediterranean, French, and Italian dishes, alongside a vast selection of tapas in the evening. Popular with the lunchtime business crowd.

394 Rue St-Jacques, 514-848-0202 **$$$**

L'Orignal

The chic cottage-style decor welcomes a trendy crowd to its *cinq à septs* to wash down canapés and oysters with excellent martinis. The warm, comfortable ambiance keeps customers coming back for the skilfully prepared seafood entrées, tuna and reindeer tartares, and wild duck dishes.

479 Rue St-Alexis, 514-303-0479,
www.restaurantlorignal.com **$$$$**

Le Garde-Manger

Le Garde-Manger is probably the splashiest, most fun restaurant in Old Montréal. The New York ambiance and the generous hosts have made this a meeting point for wired young Montrealers. The menu largely consists of a variety of seafood prepared and served in a simple and original style. Great for those who want to eat and party in the same place.

408 Rue St-François-Xavier, 514-678-5044
$$$$

Version Laurent Godbout

From the outset, Version Laurent Godbout stands out by its simple, natural decor, a presage of a true gastronomic experience. The chef serves up a highly creative Mediterranean menu. An evening of tapas and wine on the magnificent terrace,

one of the best in the city, is an unmissable Old Montréal treat.
295 Rue St-Paul Est, 514-871-9135, www.version-restaurant.com $$$$

Aszú

Aszú offers a gastronomic world tour with each bite, in perfect harmony with carefully chosen wine. Guests enjoy small dishes such as scallop ceviche, trout tartare, lamb shank or venison osso buco, in an inviting ambiance including a superb stone wall and exposed wine cellars housing a vast selection of wines by the glass. In summer, the flowered terrace is the perfect spot for lovers looking for a sensual culinary experience.
212 Rue Notre-Dame Ouest, 514-845-5436, www.aszu.ca $$$$

S Le Restaurant

A modern, elegant establishment, S Le Restaurant targets a clientele that appreciates both quality and setting. A menu with European highlights and homegrown Québec products is served. A delightful terrace is open in the summer.
125 Rue St-Paul Ouest, 514-350-1155, www.slerestaurant.com $$$$

Vauvert

Situated in the St Paul Hôtel, Vauvert offers its guests a magical trip on the Chasse-galerie, a Québec legend. The black walls, flames, and tiny white lights descending from the ceiling like fireflies enhance the underworld ambiance. The restaurant, open for lunch and dinner, offers excellent Mediterranean cuisine inspired by Québec

1. Restaurant Graziella
2. DNA Restaurant
3. Le Club Chasse et Pêche

classics. Don't miss the "fricots," their free adaptation of tapas, available in the evening only.
St Paul Hôtel, 355 Rue McGill, 514-876-2823, www.vauvert.ca **$$$$**

DNA Restaurant

Renowned for its exceptionally creative interior design, DNA Restaurant's large space is decorated with intuition and skill. To fill the space without overcrowding it, and especially to emphasize the view of the striking modernist Habitat 67 complex, certain tables are raised and surrounded by glass partitions. The intimate lounge section offers welcoming sofas and warm colours that contrast with the neutral tones of the dining room. Along with more than a dozen dishes of hand-made deli meats, the Mediterranean-themed menu has a place of honour for home-grown products. The

especially well-loved entrées are tours de force of perfectly blended flavours. Couples simply must reserve the table with a swing, which has the most breathtaking view.
355 Rue Marguerite-D'Youville, 514-287-3362, www.dnarestaurant.com **$$$$**

Restaurant Graziella

Superb Restaurant Graziella's sunny decor is harmonious and inspiring. Gastronomes and Italian cuisine aficionados will find a menu combining fresh products with both classic and innovative flavours. One could spend a whole day in this dining room with its high ceiling, magnificent cloth chandeliers and paintings by talented artists. The excellent wine list includes organic products and wines by small producers.
116 Rue McGill, 514-876-0116 **$$$$**

Da Emma

Occupying what once was Montréal's first women's prison, this restaurant's award-winning interior design is at once charming, meticulous, and chic, with massive beams and grey stones. Madame Emma's traditional Italian cuisine is worth the trip and the service is impeccable. If you're lucky enough to visit on a day that it is available, try the family speciality, tripe *alla romana*; if not, you can content yourself with a delicious dish of braised lamb and one of the best tiramisus in town.

777 Rue de la Commune Ouest, 514-392-1568
$$$$

Le Club Chasse et Pêche

The name is surprising, the decor more so: deep armchairs, kitschy lampshades, abstract photos, dark walls, all in a happy union of rustic and sophisticated – much like the menu. Claude Pelletier, the worst-kept secret of Montréal gastronomy, devises creative, refined dishes from pan-seared foie gras to rack of lamb. In summer, customers lunch on the superb flowered terrace looking out onto the Jardin du Gouverneur behind Château Ramezay.

423 Rue St-Claude, 514-861-1112,
www.leclubchasseetpeche.com **$$$$**

The Classics

Restaurant Bonaparte

Bonaparte is the perfect place for classic French cuisine in an elegant decor. Guests are seated in one of the establishment's three rooms, all richly decorated in the Empire style. The largest offers the warmth of a fireplace in winter, while another, named "La Serre" (the greenhouse), offers a subdued ambiance thanks to its many potted plants.

Auberge Bonaparte, 447 Rue St-François-Xavier, 514-844-4368, www.bonaparte.ca $$$

Le Saint-Gabriel

The attraction of the Saint-Gabriel lies above all in its enchanting decor reminiscent of early New France; the restaurant is set in an old house that served as an inn in 1754. The French and Mediterranean selections are somewhat predictable but well done.

426 Rue St-Gabriel, 514-878-3561, www.lesaint-gabriel.com $$$

Chez Queux

In an exquisite setting overlooking Place Jacques-Cartier, Chez Queux serves delicious French cuisine in a perfect classical decor. Certain dishes (grills and flambés) are prepared at the table.

158 Rue St-Paul Est, 514-866-5194, www.chezqueux.com $$$

Gibby's

Gibby's is located in an old, renovated stable. Its menu offers generous servings of beef or veal steaks served at wooden tables set around a glowing fire and surrounded by low brick-and-stone walls. In the summer months, patrons can dine comfortably outdoors in a large inner courtyard. Vegetarians beware!

298 Place D'Youville, 514-282-1837, www.gibbys.com **$$$**

Les Filles du Roy

The antique jewel of Montréal hotels, the Hostellerie Pierre du Calvet boasts one of the best dining rooms in the city. The establishment is particularly recommended for its delicious and imaginative French cuisine, which celebrates locally grown products and game. The elegant surroundings, antiques, ornamental plants and discreet service further add to the pleasure of an evening meal at the Maison Pierre du Calvet, built in 1725.

Hostellerie Pierre du Calvet, 405 Rue Bonsecours, 514-282-1725, www.pierreducalvet.ca **$$$$**

(Galerie Saint-Dizier)

Admire

Old Montréal has the city's highest density of art galleries, with no fewer than 40 galleries from the most traditional to the most avant-garde between Rue McGill and Marché Bonsecours. Here are a few that you shouldn't miss during your visit.

1. Galerie Pangée
2. Fondation DHC / Art
3. Galerie Orange

Contemporary and Avant-Garde

DHC / Art

DHC / Art is not strictly speaking an art gallery, but rather a foundation devoted since its 2007 opening to presenting major contemporary artworks from around the world and to working for a better understanding of contemporary art in the community. DHC / Art offers presentations, multimedia shows, video screenings, and accessible education for all. At least three major exhibits are featured every year. Admission is free and employees are always pleased to answer visitors' questions and discuss the art with them. Note that DHC / Art is closed on Mondays and Tuesdays. Highly recommended.

451 Rue St-Jean, 514-849-3724, www.dhc-art.org

3

Galerie Pangée

This young gallery has made a name for itself with its audacious and unconstrained choice of subjects. Both well-known and up-and-coming artists, Canadian and foreign, present innovative works, exhibits, and happenings. New projects presented on a regular basis will make you explore, discover, and see the world differently. A breath of fresh air, Pangée is more than worth the trip.

40 Rue St-Paul Ouest, 514-845-3368,
www.galeriepangee.com

Galerie Orange

Galerie Orange is the contemporary branch of Galerie Lacerte, an Old Québec City gallery that has been an institution in the Québec art market for more than 30 years. Frequently seen in international art expos, Galerie Orange actively contributes to the promotion of Canadian artists abroad. It is a serious player in the development of the visual arts in Montréal.

81 Rue St-Paul Est, 514-396-6670,
www.galerieorange.com

Galerie Saint-Dizier /
Galerie Le Royer

Galerie Saint-Dizier and its affiliated Galerie Le Royer present two different themes in superb historic buildings just steps apart. At 24 Rue St-Paul Ouest, classical and modern paintings and sculptures by mainly Québec artists are presented in a plush environment with a fireplace and grand piano. At 60 Rue St-Paul Ouest, 19th-century collections share space with pop-contemporary works. Both galleries welcome visitors with coffee or a glass of wine. Not to be missed.

Galerie Saint-Dizier: 24 Rue St-Paul Ouest, 514-845-8411, www.saintdizier.com
Galerie Le Royer: 60 Rue St-Paul Ouest, 514-287-1351, www.galerieleroyer.com

Galerie MX

Located in the Quartier International, Galerie MX offers works by well-known figures in the contemporary Montréal arts scene. The vast, beautifully designed two-story urban-style space is frequented by well-known Québec show biz personalities and presents well-publicized events year-round. Can be rented for all occasions. Worth the trip.

333 Avenue Viger Ouest, 514-315-8900, www.galeriemx.com

1. Galerie Le Royer
2. Galerie Blanche
3. Galerie MX

Galerie Blanche

In a hospitable environment that unites the classical and the modern, Galerie Blanche represents and promotes the mid-career work of figurative artists to the Montréal art market and the public at large.

218 Rue St-Paul Ouest, 514-656-3272,
www.galerieblanche.com

Atelier Art Bressan

After a career of more than 44 years, Canadian painter Pauline Bressan is known throughout Canada and abroad. Many of her works, both figurative and abstract, hang in the Musée National des Beaux-Arts du Québec and in some of the most prestigious private collections in the country. Atelier Art Bressan presents works by this talented artist and by her daughter Emmanuelle Bressan.

206 / R2 Rue St-Paul Ouest, 514-842-1055,
www.artbressan.com

1. La Guilde Graphique
2. Galerie Lamoureux Ritzenhoff

Traditional Galleries

Galerie G2K / Galerie 2000

Galerie G2K presents a record number of artists, with works for all tastes and budgets in its two exhibition spaces. It also offers a framing service and free worldwide delivery.

Division Vieux-Montréal: *45 Rue St-Paul Ouest, 514-844-1812*
Division Palais des Congrès: *1001 Place Jean-Paul-Riopelle, 514-868-6668, www.gallery2000.ca*

Galerie Lamoureux Ritzenhoff

The Galerie Lamoureux Ritzenhoff represents artists who have made their careers in Canada. The works from some twenty contemporary artists hang alongside those of masters such as Marc-Aurèle Fortin, Stanley Cosgrove, Clarence Gagnon, Cornelius Krieghoff, and Jean Paul Riopelle. The gallery also offers a useful on-line store.

68 Rue St-Paul Ouest, 514-840-9066, www.galerielamoureuxritzenhoff.com

Le Bourget / Le Luxart

Almost next door neighbours, Le Bourget and Le Luxart are affiliated galleries that offer a vast range of figurative, classic and modern works by more than 50 Québec and Canadian artists. Some of the paintings on offer make beautiful souvenirs of a visit to the city, such as scenes of snow-covered streets or works depicting Montréal's lively festivals; other smaller paintings are reasonably priced to buy as a gift.

Le Bourget: 34 Rue St-Paul Ouest, Suite B, 514-845-2525, www.galerielebourget.com
Le Luxart: 66 Rue St-Paul Ouest, 514-848-8944

La Guilde Graphique

The charming and welcoming Guilde Graphique mainly offers prints, engravings, and other works on paper, selected with great sensitivity. There are also some tasteful, high-quality Canadiana canvases. The works are affordable and the format is perfect for a visitor's suitcase.

9 Rue St-Paul Ouest, 514-844-3438,
www.guildegraphique.com

5

(Scandinave Les Bains Vieux-Montréal)

Indulge

Old Montréal is a wonderful setting for extraordinary wellness centres that pamper body and soul. During your trip, enjoy the complete bliss of a body care session or yoga workshop for profound relaxation and renewed energy.

1

Pamper Yourself

Spa Zazen

More than just a spa, Zazen is a holistic clinic combining alternative medicine, traditional Asian care, yoga and Pilates courses, and therapeutic massages and energy work. The natural, Zen-inspired design bathes the spa in a peaceful aura. Organic products are used in care and massages.

209 Rue St-Paul Ouest, 3rd floor, 514-287-1772, www.spazazen.com

Valmont Beauty Lounge

This sunny lounge decorated with artworks in a historic building offers well-being based on Asian techniques. Clients can enjoy yoga, reflexology, reiki, hot stone massage, and nutrition consultations.

446 Rue Ste-Hélène, 514-510-6850, www.evalmont.com

Le Spa de l'Hôtel Le St-James

With its magnificent stone wall decorated with candles and its sparkling marble surroundings, Le Spa de l'Hôtel Le St-James distinguishes itself with its magical, romantic atmosphere and its unrivalled intimacy. Clients enjoy a private bathroom with a sauna, a multiple-jet shower, and a steam room. Services include hot stone

1. Valmont Beauty Lounge
2. Rainspa
3. Le Spa de l'Hôtel Le St-James

and rain massages, complete exfoliation, and a body wrap in rasul, a type of clay rich in iron oxide and magnesium. Most services are also offered to couples.

Hôtel Le St-James, 355 Rue St-Jacques, 514-841-3111, www.hotellestjames.com

Rainspa

The impeccable natural décor of Rainspa in the Hôtel Place d'Armes enwraps guests in Mediterranean warmth. Rainspa's non-traditional Turkish bath, with its stimulating eucalyptus steam, offers an exotic experience. Services include massages for pregnant women, violet clay massage, hammam-style gommage, and exfoliation with mineral-rich Dead Sea salts.

Le Place d'Armes Hôtel & Suites, 55 Rue St-Jacques, 514-282-2727, www.rainspa.ca

Laïlama Santé Beauté

In a pleasant, calm, and discreet centre, Laïlama Laqubi offers a range of therapeutic and beauty care with savoir-faire and professionalism, including ayurvedic massage with gotu kola oil, Mongolian massage, and natural exfoliating depilation with honey or sugar.

204 Rue Notre-Dame Ouest, Suite 100, 514-288-9508, www.lailama.com

1

Glam Salon Boutique

The stylists in this well-designed salon are passionate creators at the cutting edge of all fashion trends and skilled in European cut and colour techniques.

364 Rue St-Paul Ouest, 514-499-0601,
www.glamsalonboutique.com

Scandinave Les Bains
Vieux-Montréal

Thermotherapy, a concept related to Scandinavian baths, is simple and effective: heating the body in a dry or moist sauna followed by a reviving cool shower or Nordic bath and ending in a moment of complete relaxation. Faithful to the theme, the contemporary design of Scandinave Les Bains brings together warm (wood) and cold (stone and marble) materials to create a calm, dignified environment. Besides the baths, there are rest areas for languorous relaxation, a juice bar, and more than a dozen massage rooms. Note that the fee for a massage includes unlimited access to the baths. Clients who prefer to use only the baths have 2hrs to enjoy them.

71 Rue de la Commune Ouest, 514-288-2009,
www.scandinavemontreal.com

1. Glam Salon Boutique
2. Scandinave Les Bains Vieux-Montréal
3. Centre Luna Yoga

Get Yourself Moving

Gymnasia

The superb training studio Gymnasia offers individual yoga and spinning classes and a sunny, well-equipped gym. A natural food and supplements bar and massage and osteopathy treatments are also available. Friendly, personal service.

203 Place D'Youville, 514-288-9412, www.gymnasia.biz

Centre Luna Yoga

Open to all, Centre Luna Yoga gives a series of courses and workshops based on the lively, dynamic Vinyasa style of yoga. Not to be missed are the free courses at each full moon and the candlelight sessions on Thursdays from 5pm to 7pm. Therapeutic Thai massage is also offered.

231 Rue St-Paul Ouest, Suite 200, 514-845-1881, www.centrelunayoga.com

Centre Yoga Plus

With a wide range of services including individual sessions and multidisciplinary workshops, Centre Yoga Plus offers a rejuvenating workout at the heart of Old Montréal. The unique workshops include detox and qigong yoga.

372 Rue Notre-Dame Ouest, 514-848-9301, www.centreyogaplus.com

École Satyam de Hata Yoga

Infused with a spiritual approach, École Satyam teaches hatha yoga in the pure Indian tradition. Yoga courses and workshops for beginners and experts and meditation sessions are offered in a warm environment at affordable prices.

110 Rue McGill, Suite 201, 514-861-1296, www.yogasatyam.com

6

(Clusier Habilleur)

Shop

In Old Montréal's narrow streets, window shopping transforms into a sensory, cultural experience. Uncover avant-garde fashion and design creations by prominent Montréal designers, browse through elegant boutiques, and discover original concepts and the cream of Québécois and Aboriginal crafts.

1. Noël Éternel
2. Papeterie Casse-Noisette
3. Librissime

Specialized and Surprising

Canadian Music Centre

The Canadian Music Centre is a music library in which visitors can consult a large collection of works and scores by Canadian composers. A selection of CDs and scores is for sale.

416 Rue McGill, 514-866-3477,
www.centremusique.ca

Joseph Ponton Costumes

No fewer than 15,000 costumes are available for sale or rent in this fantasy boutique in Old Montréal. It's worth a trip for the sheer pleasure of discovery! Custom crafting is also available.

480 Rue St-François-Xavier, 514-849-3238,
www.pontoncostumes.com

Librissime

This magnificent European-style bookstore is a dream for lovers of fine books. Collectible books, rare and limited editions, and reading accessories and gifts.

62 Rue St-Paul Ouest, 514-841-0123,
www.librissime.com

3

Noël Éternel

A Christmas wonderland even at the height of summer, Noël Éternel sells Russian decorations, Italian nativity scenes, German and Polish glass ornaments, and decorative village scenes in numerous themes (such as New England, the mountains, New York, or the North Pole).
461 Rue St-Sulpice, 514-285-4944,
www.noeleternel.com

Papeterie Casse-Noisette

This charming shop offers an impressive choice of letter papers, including sublime stationery hand-crafted in Québec. It also offers a great assortment of fountain pens, greeting cards, leather-bound notebooks, Santons de Charlevoix (traditional Québec nativity scenes), and original paintings displayed in a small mezzanine.
445 Rue St-Sulpice, 514-845-4980

Univers Toutou

This interactive shop allows children to create their own plush toys. Staff help children choose a toy, stuff it (hug testing included), give it a soul by making a wish, dress it, and create a passport for it before making a promise of unconditional love.
503 Place d'Armes, 514-288-2599,
www.universtoutou.com

1. Mortimer Snodgrass
2. 12° en Cave
3. Atelier-Boutique Gogo Glass

Mortimer Snodgrass

There's something for everyone at Mortimer Snodgrass, including every delightfully useless and strikingly original gift idea you could imagine and a superb collection of accessories and toys for babies and children. For the humorous gift-giver in search of that perfect catch.

209 Rue St-Paul Ouest, 514-499-2851, http://shop.mortimersnodgrass.com

12° en Cave

If you've decided to set up a wine cellar in your home, drop by 12° en Cave; you'll find everything an expert wine taster may need, from glasses and vineyard maps to hygrometers and store-rooms.

367 Rue St-Paul Est, 514-866-5722, www.12encave.com

Handcrafts and Artworks

Atelier-Boutique Gogo Glass

Annie Michaud's blown glass creations, such as citrus juicers and salt cellars, are both luminous and ingenious. If you're lucky, you may be able to see this talented glass blower working on site.

Marché Bonsecours, 385 Rue de la Commune, 514-397-8882, www.anniemichaud.com

Galerie Elca London Art Inuit

Lovers of Inuit art will enjoy stopping by the impressive Elca London gallery, where numerous artists from the Canadian North present wonderful collections of engravings and sculptures.

224 Rue St-Paul Ouest, 514-282-1173, www.elcalondon.com

Le Chariot

Le Chariot exhibits fantastic artworks by Inuit and other native peoples, which are also sold here. It is really worth visiting just to take a look.

446 Place Jacques-Cartier, 514-875-6134, www.galerielechariot.com

L'Empreinte coopérative

Set up in a historic building in Vieux-Montréal, L'Empreinte is a Québec artisan co-op that sells fashion accessories, clothing, artwork and decorative household objects. This is a good spot to discover the latest trends in Québec arts and crafts.

272 Rue St-Paul Est, 514-861-4427, www.lempreintecoop.com

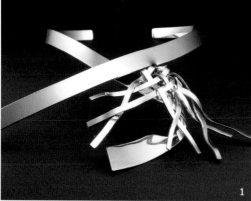

1. Jewelry from Roland Dubuc
2. Marché Bonsecours
3. Marché du Vieux

Roland Dubuc

This innovative jeweller's workshop-boutique is definitely worth a visit. His quality unique and limited-edition creations, made from minutely worked, folded, and textured gold and silver, draw on origami and sculpture techniques. Visitors can watch Roland Dubuc at work in his workshop and learn about his crafting process.

163 Rue Saint-Paul Ouest, 514-844-1221, www.rolanddubuc.com

Marché Bonsecours

The Bonsecours market is the place to shop for crafts and exclusive designer items. Among the boutiques-galeries to visit, keep in mind the Galerie des métiers d'art *(514-878-2787)* and the Boutique Arts en mouvement *(514-875-9717)*.

390 Rue St-Paul Est, 514-878-2787, www2.ville.montreal.qc.ca/marchebonsecours

Les Artisans du Meuble Québécois

The craftspeople at Les Artisans du Meuble Québécois create new antique-style furniture that blends in well with the decor of modern houses.

88 Rue St-Paul Est, 514-866-1836

3

Gourmet Foods

Les Délices de l'Érable

This little dessert restaurant is based on a very interesting concept: a boutique selling a panoply of maple products, a small museum of maple cultivation with syrup tasting in summer, and a counter selling treats such as gelatos and sorbets all sweetened with maple syrup.

84 Rue St-Paul Est, express counter at 87 Rue de la Commune, 514-765-3456, mapledelights.com

Marché du Vieux

Marché du Vieux offers a vast, attractive selection of home-grown Québec products. Attractive gift baskets can be prepared for you. The little attached bistro offers a light menu along with coffee and pastries.

8 Rue St-Paul Est, 514-393-2772, www.marcheduvieux.com

Ateliers et Saveurs

Ateliers et Saveurs is an ingenious concept that will delight gourmets. First a boutique selling fine European food products such as truffle oil, this cheerfully decorated space offers culinary workshops for all levels, for those wishing to uncover the secrets of gastronomy or improve their skills in the kitchen.

444 Rue St-Francois-Xavier, 514-849-2866, www.atelieretsaveurs.com

Fashion

Ambre

Ambre presents exclusive haute-couture women's fashions by Montréal and European designers. The welcoming staff offer personalized service.

201 Rue St-Paul Ouest, 514-982-0325

Boutique DG3

Celebrating the creativity of Québec designers, Boutique DG3 (Diffusion Griff 3000) sells some thirty collections for men and women, as well as accessories.

Marché Bonsecours, 350 Rue St-Paul Est, 514-866-2006, www.diffusiongriff3000.com

Clusier Habilleur

If you want an enriching, even educational shopping experience, meet with one of the unpretentious stylists at Clusier Habilleur. You'll learn more about urban ready-to-wear fashion and enjoy unparalleled personalized service. In addition to top-notch contemporary collections with impeccable fabrics and cuts, clothes can be made to measure.

46 Rue McGill, 514-842-1717, www.clusier.com

Michel Brisson

This elegant, contemporary shop offers top-of-the-line menswear with refined, clean lines and a wonderful selection of shoes.

384 Rue St-Paul Ouest, 514-285-1012, www.michelbrisson.com

1. Boutique DG3
2. Delano Design

Delano Design

This gallery-boutique embodies the essence of Montréal creativity in women's fashion, furniture, and visual arts. The welcoming shop is actually lit from under brilliantly coloured canvases by artist Tannous. This permanent exhibit sets the tone for the generous and enthusiastic welcome by staff who know each designer's creations inside and out. Collections include apparel, accessories (handbags, belts, and jewellery), furniture, and decorations, mostly from well-known or up-and-coming Montréal creators.

70 Rue St-Paul Ouest, 514-286-5005,
www.delanodesign.com

Boutique Reborn

Style, quality, and fantastic things are on offer in this tiny boutique, more like a corridor than a storefront. Some pieces by Montréal designers, but mainly exclusive creations and collections by European stylists.

231 Rue St-Paul Ouest, 514-499-8549,
www.reborn.ws

Design

Le Baldaquin Montréal

Prestigious Le Baldaquin Montréal is known for its vast collection of design and decorative items, bath, table, and bed linens, and exceptional-quality furniture. The unique motifs, exotic textures, and graceful lines are a feast for the eyes.

63 Rue de la Commune Ouest, 514-288-6366, www.lebaldaquinmontreal.com

Bonaldo

Whatever the thickness of your wallet, have a look at Bonaldo. Retro design lovers will be bowled over by the fantastic works on offer – unique furniture and decorations, always inspiring and attractive.

2 Rue Le Royer, 514-287-9222, www.bonaldo.ca

1. Option D
2. Le Baldaquin Montréal
3. Bonaldo

Option D

Option D is full of wonderful finds celebrating the culinary arts. These contemporary accents by Québécois and European designers are original and high-quality.

50 Rue St-Paul Ouest, 514-842-7117, www.optiond.ca

Saïthong

This exotic Asian-themed boutique offers a superb collection of apparel, accessories, shoes, and curiosities. Worth a visit for its fabulous silk garments and its handbags, unusually original and affordable.

366 Rue Notre-Dame Ouest, 514-843-5819, www.saithongimport.com

Step Out

Under the fairytale lights frosting the beautiful architecture of yesterday and today, Old Montréal's nightlife is resolutely urban and modern. From trendy lounges to romantic wine bars, from pubs to uninhibited *boîtes à chansons*, the range of remarkable night spots is sure to provide a memorable evening on the town.

1. Suite 701 – Lounge
2. Grange vin + bouffe
3. Le Confessionnal

Stylish Apéro Bars

Business Lounge and Tapas

The unmissable *cinq à septs* bring young professionals in all their finery out for tapas and cocktails at Business in a retro-chic ambiance that heats up as the evening progresses. The decor reveals original finds such as lamps made of naked, lightbulbs suspended from the ceiling in frames. Big names spin from Thursday to Saturday.

211 Rue Notre-Dame Ouest, 514-658-1526

Suite 701 – Lounge / Terrasse

The former lobby of the Hôtel Place d'Armes has been transformed into a polished, contemporary lounge with huge windows. The quality of the cocktails and the professional and personal service draw a tony clientele for drinks and snacks after work. Cocktail hour tends to go on rather longer than an hour, and in the evenings a DJ presides on the balcony over the room. Suite 701 – Lounge is also well-known for its bartenders' skills; it is one of the rare establishments where the staff mix cocktails free-hand (and skilfully!). The terrace of Aix restaurant is available to lounge customers and offers a great view of the city, one of the best places to watch the fireworks of the L'International des Feux Loto-Québec on Saturdays and Wednesdays from mid-June to mid-August.

Place d'Armes Hôtel & Suites, 701 Côte de la Place-d'Armes, 514-904-1201, www.suite701.com

Grange vin + bouffe

The marvellous central bar of Grange vin + bouffe transforms this resolutely urban establishment into a comfortable wine bar. The contemporary design is festooned with rustic decorations: natural wood, cowskin patterns on the stools, wagon-wheel lamps, and stuffed deer trophies. The effect is surprisingly successful and entices clients to extend their wine tasting experience. More than thirty wines from all parts of the world, including private imports, are sold by the glass and are perfect matches to the snack menu.

120 Rue McGill, 514-394-9463,
www.grangeresto.ca

Le Confessionnal

Le Confessionnal's comfortable little lounge is the perfect spot to get to know the gilded professional youth of Montréal. Cocktail hour is so popular that there's sometimes a line, and once inside, getting to the bar is a matter of elbows. A little bit farther inside, the dance floor is filled with swaying, suited bodies.

431 Rue McGill, 514-656-1350,
www.confessionnal.ca

Verses Sky

Ideally located on the roof of Hôtel Nelligan, Verses Sky boasts one of Old Montréal's most delightful terraces. Perfect for catching a few rays during cocktail hour while savouring a glass of the surprising house sangria and enjoying a quick bite.

Hôtel Nelligan, 100 Rue St-Paul Ouest,
514-788-4000

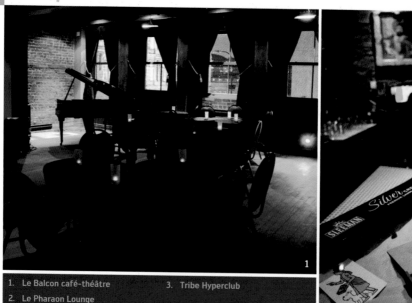

1. Le Balcon café-théâtre
2. Le Pharaon Lounge
3. Tribe Hyperclub

Warm Ambiances

Le Balcon café-théâtre

This plush, intimate room hosts varied dinner theatre shows combining visual arts, music, and theatre. Dinner includes a four-course table d'hôte.
304 Rue Notre-Dame Est, 514-528-9766,
www.lebalcon.ca

Le Pharaon Lounge

Connected to the *Tintin* themed Le Petit Moulinsart restaurant, the warm, unpretentious Le Pharaon Lounge offers a vast selection of Belgian beers and a festive crowd of regulars. A good place to get a feel for the local atmosphere.
Le Petit Moulinsart, 139 Rue St-Paul Ouest,
514-843-4779, www.lepetitmoulinsart.com/pharaon

Narcisse Bistro + Bar à vin

L'Auberge du Vieux-Port houses the refined but comfortable Narcisse Bistro + Bar à vin. Along with nightly jazz concerts from Thursday to Saturday, the house offers an excellent wine list and a delicious menu made from market ingredients in an intimate, plush dining room. Narcisse has two pleasant terraces, one overlooking Rue de la Commune and the other on the roof, with a spectacular view of the river and the neighbourhood.
Auberge du Vieux-Port, 97 Rue de la Commune
Est, 514-876-0081, www.narcissebistro.com

Les Deux Pierrots

Les Deux Pierrots is a veritable Montréal institution that has always lived up to its clients' taste in entertainment. If your idea of a fun night out entails

3

drinking beer and standing on your chair to sing Québécois pop and folk songs, this is the place for you. Even if not, you'd still do well to stop in. Those who do not speak French may not get everything that's going on, but they will get a taste of a certain type of traditional Québécois nightlife; the lively atmosphere here is contagious. And you'll enjoy the experience even more if you make it a group outing. Pleasant terrace in summer.

104 Rue St-Paul Est, 514-861-1270,
www.lespierrots.com

Pub St-Paul

Le Pub St-Paul is best-known for its shows, although it also offers a simple menu. The glazed second-floor room overlooks the river and the Old Port. The main attractions are the welcoming ambiance and the good prices. Le Pub St-Paul's clientele comes for the live music at high volumes. Cover for shows Fridays and Saturdays.

124 Rue St-Paul Est, 514-874-0485,
www.pubstpaul.com

Tribe Hyperclub

Just as you'd expect from a place that calls itself a "hyperclub": a lineup at the door, cellphones glued to ears, revellers seeing and being seen, large doormen letting you in as though it's a privilege, and thundering music that will leave your ears buzzing till Monday, spun by the biggest names in house music. For serious clubbers.

300 Rue St-Jacques, 514-845-3066,
www.tribehyperclub.com

1. Aszú
2. Terrasse 701

Terraces

Old Montréal boasts some magnificent terraces. Whether they're discrete backyard haunts or trendy rooftop decks, they offer the ideal setting for a cocktail between friends, a romantic meal or a magical night out with a stunning view of the river.

For Lunch

Boris Bistro (see p. 74)
Le Club Chasse et Pêche (see p. 83)

For Cocktails

Terrasse 701 (see p. 114)
Jardin Nelson (see p. 74)
Narcisse Bistro + Bar à vin (see p. 116)
Verses Sky (see p. 115)

For Dinner

Aszú (see p. 81)
Gibby's (see p. 85)
S Le Restaurant (see p. 81)
Version Laurent Godbout (see p. 80)

Getting There and Around

By Car

Private parking lots are numerous in Old Montréal, but are moderately expensive ($4/hr and $10/day). Parking on the street ($3/hr) is possible, but be sure to read the signs carefully. Ticketing of illegally parked cars is strict and expensive.

By Bus or Metro

Visitors are strongly advised to take advantage of Montréal's public transportation system, which consists of an extensive network of buses and subway trains (the metro), operated by the **Société de Transport de Montréal (STM)**, that serve the region well. Old Montréal is served by Square-Victoria, Place-d'Armes, and Champ-de-Mars metro stations, and by bus lines 515, 55, and 14.

Visitors can purchase single tickets at $2.75 each. For bus schedules, dial 514-288-6287 (A-U-T-O-B-U-S). For all other information, visit *www.stm.info* or call 514-786-4636.

On Foot

Old Montréal is an easy area to get around. Its north-south and east-west grid of streets makes an almost perfect checkerboard.

The east-west arteries are divided by Boulevard Saint-Laurent, where street numbers begin at zero and increase eastward and westward, with the direction usually designated in the address (*est* and *ouest*).

Tourist Information

Old Montréal Tourist Welcome Office

Jun to Sep every day 9am to 7pm, Sep to May Wed-Sun 9am to 1pm and 2pm to 5pm
174 Rue Notre-Dame Est (corner of Place Jacques-Cartier)
Champ-de-Mars metro, 514-874-1696

Guided Tours

There are several guided tours highlighting the different aspects of Old Montréal through various themes. For example, **Montréal Ghosts** *(514-868-0303 or 877-868-0303, www.fantommontreal. com)*, with their renowned **Ghosts of Old Montréal** tour, invites you to discover Old Montréal's legends, famous characters and historic crimes.

The **Old Montréal Walking Tour** *(514-844-4021, www.guidatour.qc.ca)* reveals the history, architecture, and legends of Old Montréal.

Amphitour *($32; May to late Oct; departure on the corner of Rue de la Commune and Boule-vard St-Laurent, 514-849-5181, www.montreal-amphibus-tour.com)* offers guided tours of Old Montréal (on land) and the Old Port (on the water) aboard an amphibious bus. A treat for kids!

A **calèche (horse-drawn carriage) station** is located on Place d'Armes. Ask one of the coachmen about a romantic and informative calèche ride through Old Montréal – or just admire the horses.

Festivals and Events

February

Montréal High Lights Festival

late Feb to early Mar, 514-288-9955 or 888-477-9955, www.montrealenlumiere.com
The Montréal High Lights Festival brings a bit of magic to the dead of the Québec winter. Light shows draw attention to the city's architecture, and fireworks are presented. In the Arts de la Table part of the festival, top chefs from all over the world offer samples, meals and workshops. The festival also showcases concerts, dance and theatre.

Montréal Fashion Week

www.montrealfashionweek.ca

The Montréal Fashion Week takes place in early March at Marché Bonsecours. A major event for fashion fanatics, it showcases renowned designers from Québec and around the world.

May

Pointe-à-Callière's Cultural Feast

Pointe-à-Callière, Montréal Museum of Archaeology and History, 514-872-9150,
www.pacmusee.qc.ca

A celebration of Montréal's cooking heritage and cultures, the Cultural Feast is held on Place Royale, with stands offering delicious culinary specialties, dishes, and sweets. Shows and games are also offered.

June

Montréal Baroque

www.montrealbaroque.com

During four days in late June, the Montréal Baroque music festival presents works dating from the Middle Ages and the Renaissance, with some concerts taking place in the Chapelle Notre-Dame-de-Bon-Secours.

June to August

L'International des Feux Loto-Québec

late June to early Aug, 514-397-2000, www.montrealfeux.com

L'International des Feux Loto-Québec, an international fireworks competition, invites the world's top pyrotechnic artists to La Ronde (on Île Sainte-Hélène) to compete in presenting high-quality pyro-musical shows. Presentations take places at 10pm every Saturday in June and every Wednesday and Saturday in July. Montrealers head to the amusement park (where admission fees must be paid), the Pont Jacques-Cartier, the riverbanks or a terrace in Old Montréal (free) to admire the spectacular fireworks displays that illuminate the sky above the city.

August

Pointe-à-Callière's 18th-Century Public Market

Pointe-à-Callière, Montréal Museum of Archaeology and History, 514-872-9150,
www.pacmusee.qc.ca

This joyful recreation of Montréal's first public market (1750), bringing together farmers, craftspeople, musicians, and storytellers, is definitely worth a stop. This public market, held the last week of August, offers tastings of traditional foods, musical shows, a recreated Aboriginal camp, reenactments of historical scenes, and activities for children such as costumes and period games.

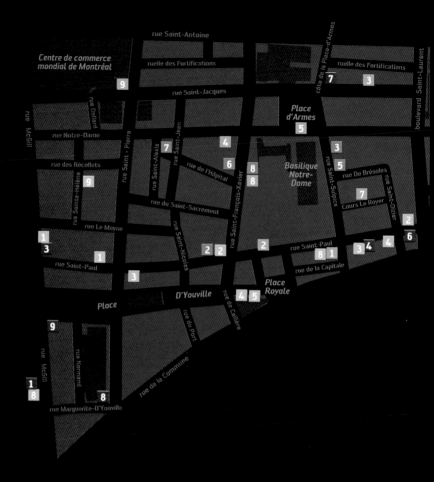

If you're into avant-garde culture and design, check out these nerve centres of the bubbling, lively audacity of Montréal creativity.

1   Brunch at **Le Cartet** (see p. 78)
2   A visit to **DHC / ART** (see p. 88)
3   A coffee break at **Nomad Station** (see p. 71)
4 and 5 Window shopping at **Delano Design** (see p. 109) and **Bonaldo** (see p. 110)
6   Vernissages at the art galleries on **Rue Saint-Paul** (see p. 90)
7   Cocktails at **Suite 701 – Lounge** (see p. 114)
8   Dinner at **DNA Restaurant** (see p. 82)
9   A night at the **St Paul Hôtel** (see p. 62)

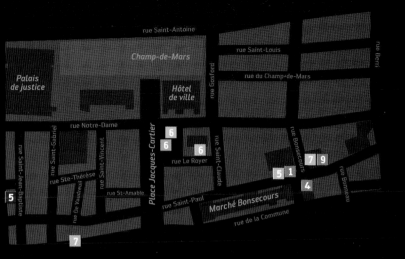

Tailor-Made Itineraries

For Hedonists

As if tailor-made to appeal to the hedonist in you, Old Montréal will tantalize your senses. Whether it's beautiful decorations, gourmet cuisine, or complete relaxation you're after, you're in the right place!

1   Brunch at **Holder** (see p. 75)
2   Massage or energy work at **Spa Zazen** (see p. 96)
3   Window shopping at **Marché de la Villette** (see p. 73)
4   A visit to the **Galerie Pangée** (see p. 89)
5   Window shopping at **12° en Cave** (see p. 104)
6   A peaceful break in the **Jardin du Gouverneur** (see p. 40)
7   Cocktails on the terrace of **Narcisse Bistro + Bar à vin** (see p. 116)
8   Dinner at **Restaurant Graziella** (see p. 82)
9   A night at the **Hôtel Gault** (see p. 60)

For Lovers

A romantic refuge where every gentle, attentive extra touch is at your service, Old Montréal is for lovers above all. Don't be shy; it's all there to be enjoyed – together.

1   Breakfast in the courtyard of **Hôtel Nelligan** (see p. 61)
2   A visit to **Roland Dubuc**'s jewellery workshop-boutique (see p. 106)
3   Couple's relaxation in the Turkish bath at **Rainspa** (see p. 97)
4   Lunch on the terrace at **Azsú** (see p. 81)
5 and 6 A **calèche** ride with a stop at the flower kiosk in **Place Jacques-Cartier** (see p. 35)
7   A stolen kiss in the pedestrian area of **Cours Le Royer** (see p. 25)
8   Cocktails and dinner on the terrace at **Restaurant Bonaparte** (see p. 84)
9   A night at the **Hôtel Le St-James** (see p. 66)

For Inquiring Minds

History and culture buffs who want to discover the secrets of the art of living in Old Montréal will enjoy this mind-expanding tour.

1   Breakfast at **Olive + Gourmando** (see p. 70)
2   A visit to **La Guilde Graphique** (see p. 93)
3   A pilgrimage to **Librissime** (see p. 102)
4   A visit to the **Pointe-à-Callière** museum (see p. 26)
5   Lunch at **L'Arrivage** (see p. 73)
6   A reading break on **Place De La Dauversière** (see p. 38)
7   Dinner at **Les Filles du Roy** (see p. 85)
8   A night at the **Hôtel Nelligan** (see p. 61)

For the Offbeat

Amazing finds are in store for travellers looking for the out-of-the-ordinary. This selection of Old Montréal's original, unique boutiques, museums, and restaurants offers original experiences to startle and delight.

1   Brunch at **Marché Serafim** (see p. 72)
2 and 3 A visit to **Mortimer Snodgrass** (see p. 104) and **Noël Éternel** (see p. 103)
4   A visit to the **Musée Marguerite-Bourgeoys** (see p. 46)
5   The tea ceremony at **Ming Tao Xuan** (see p. 70)
6   A rummage through **Joseph Ponton Costumes** (see p. 102)
7   Dinner at **L'Orignal** (see p. 80)
8   A guided ***Ghosts of Old Montréal*** tour (see p. 120)
9   A night at **Hostellerie Pierre du Calvet** (see p. 64)

Index

Admire

Indulge

Shop

Step Out

Tourist Information

Photo Credits

Cover Page

From top to bottom and from left to right:

Rue Saint-Paul, Sylvain Cousineau; Hôtel Gault interior, Hôtel Gault; the bar at Version Laurent Godbout, Bill Friedlander; Delano Design shop, Thierry Ducharme; the terrace at Club Chasse et Pêche, conception-photo.com; Galerie Pangée, Michael Flomen.

Inside Pages

Pages 4-5: Camilo Gómez-Durán; *pages 6-7:* Oriane Meyer; *page 8:* Samuel Charland; *page 13:* 1 Éric Turgeon, 2 Sylvain Cousineau; *pages 14-15:* Graham Hughes; *pages 16-17:* 1 Stefania Rossi, 2 Graham Hughes, 3 Anthony Luckban; *pages 18-19:* Denis Tremblay; *pages 20-21:* 1 Philippe Côté-Léger, 2 & 3 Sara Bourgoin; *pages 22-23:* Raul Dario Acosta; *page 24:* 1 Michel Marcoux, 2 Paola Andrea Valfredi Mendoza, 3 Robert Régimbald; *page 27:* 1 Joël Labbé, 2 Thierry Ducharme; *pages 28-29:* 1 Louise Jasmin, 2 Denis Farley, Collaboration: Claude Cormier/architectes paysagistes inc., Groupe Cardinal Hardy; *pages 30-31:* 1 David Bellavance Ricard, 2 Thierry Ducharme; *page 33:* 1 Sylvain Cousineau, 2 David Bellavance Ricard; *pages 34-35:* 1 Thierry Ducharme, 2 Lorraine Deslauriers; *pages 36-37:* 1 Bill Friedlander, 2 Yves Bouchard; *page 39:* Olivier Blouin; *pages 40-41:* 1 David Bellavance Ricard, 2 Jim Royal, 3 Maxime Sun; *page 43:* 1 David Bellavance Ricard, 2 & 3 Thierry Ducharme; *pages 44-45:* 1 Yves Bouchard, 2 Thierry Ducharme; *pages 46-47:* 1 Thierry Ducharme, 2 Geneviève M. Santerre, 3 Lorraine Deslauriers; *pages 48-49:* Olivier Blouin; *pages 50-51:* Arturo de Grandmont; *pages 52-53:* 1 Luc Charron, 2 Geneviève M. Santerre, 3 Jean Fiset, 4. Stefania Rossi; *pages 54-55:* 1 Camilo Gómez-Durán, 2 Robert Régimbald, 3 Olivier Blouin; *pages 56-57:* 1 Yves Bouchard, 2 Samuel Charland, 3 Camilo Gómez-Durán; *page 58:* St. Paul Hôtel/Jean Blais photographer; *pages 60-61:* 1 Thierry Ducharme, 2 & 3 Hôtel Gault; *pages 62-63:* 1 Graphipack Inc. for Groupe Antonopoulos, 2 Thierry Ducharme, 3 St. Paul Hôtel/Jean Blais photographer; *pages 64-65:* 1 Hostellerie Pierre du Calvet, 2 Graphipack Inc. for Groupe Antonopoulos; *pages 66-67:* 1 Thierry Ducharme, 2 & 3 Hôtel Le St-James; *page 68:* Nicolas Ruel; *pages 70-71:* 1 Joey Lee, 2 & 3 Thierry Ducharme; *pages 72-73:* 1 Thierry Ducharme, 2 Éric Girard, 3 Thierry Ducharme; *pages 74-75:* 1 & 2 Thierry Ducharme, 3 Jean-Marc Lebeau; *pages 76-77:* 1, 2 & 3 Thierry Ducharme; *pages 78-79:* 1 Chez l'Épicier, 2 Barroco; *pages 80-81:* 1 S Le Restaurant, 2 Aszú, 3 Restaurant Vauvert; *pages 82-83:* 1 Restaurant Graziella, 2 DNA Restaurant, 3 conception-photo.com; *pages 84-85:* 2 Thierry Ducharme, 2 Les Filles du Roy; *page 86:* Galerie Saint-Dizier; *pages 88-89:* 1 Michael Flomen, 2 George Fok, 3 Guy L'Heureux; *pages 90-91:* 1 Galerie Saint-Dizier, 2 Galerie Blanche, 3 Olivier Malenfant Photographer; *pages 92-93:* 1 Jacqueline Martin, 2 Thierry Ducharme; *page 94:* Scandinave Les Bains Vieux-Montréal; *pages 96-97:* 1 Nicolas Dupéré/Nico-World, 2 Graphipack Inc. for Groupe Antonopoulos, 3 Hôtel Le St-James; *pages 98-99:* 1 Thierry Ducharme, 2 Scandinave Les Bains Vieux-Montréal, 3 Bram Levinson; *page 100:* pbi Design; *pages 102-103:* 1 Urvi Shah, 2 Thierry Ducharme, 3 Ubique Média/Jean-Philippe Brochu; *pages 104-105:* 1 & 2 Thierry Ducharme, 3 Marc Montplaisir; *pages 106-107:* 1 Roland Dubuc, 2 Thierry Ducharme, 3 Marché du Vieux; *pages 108-109:* 1 & 2 Thierry Ducharme; *pages 110-111:* 1 Thierry Ducharme, 2 Pierre Bélanger, 3 Bonaldo; *page 112:* Bill Friedlander; *pages 114-115:* 1 Groupe Antonopoulos, 2 Thierry Ducharme, 3 Le Confessionnal; *pages 116-117:* 1 Le Balcon café-théâtre, 2 Thierry Ducharme, 3 Tribe Hyperclub; *page 118:* 1 Aszú, 2 conception-photo.com; *page 119:* Marcin Wozniak; *pages 120-121:* Thierry Ducharme; *page 128:* Graham Hughes.